Life's But A Game:

Go With The Flow!

A Spiritual Book For Today's Teenagers And Young Adults

By Eileen McCourt

Life's But a Game! Go With the Flow!

A Spiritual Manual for Teenagers and Young Adults

By Eileen McCourt

Life's But a Game! Go With the Flow! A Spiritual Manual for Teenagers and Young Adults. This book was first published in Great Britain in paperback during March 2016.

The moral right of Eileen McCourt is to be identified as the author of this work and has been asserted by her in accordance with the Copyright, Designs and Patents Act of 1988.

All rights are reserved and no part of this book may be produced or utilized in any format, or by any means, electronic or mechanical, including photocopying, recording or by any information storage or retrieval system, without prior permission in writing from the publishers – Coast & Country/Ads2life. ads2life@btinternet.com

All rights reserved.

ISBN-13: 978-1523832712

Copyright © March 2016 Eileen McCourt

Contents

                                                                         Page

About the Author	i
Acknowledgements	v
Reviews	vii
Foreword	ix

PART ONE: THE WONDER OF YOU!

Chpt. 1: Who am I?	1
Your physical body	1
Your five physical senses	2
Beyond your physical senses	4
Your Spiritual body	5
Feeding your Soul	7
Now you know!	8
Chpt. 2: Where have I come from?	9
Reincarnation	9
Eternity	10
Chpt. 3: Why am I here?	12
Earth school	13
Collecting brownie points	13
Free will	15
Planning your life	16
Your parents	21
Learning the lessons	23

  Page

Being true to yourself 24
Life review 28
The merry-go-round of life! 29

PART TWO: THE WONDER OF GOD!

Chpt. 4:   We've got God all wrong! 30
What God is NOT 31

Chpt. 5:   Who or what is God? 35
We are all energy 35
Energy is always moving and changing 38
Divorce and separation 39
What happens when we die? 41
The silver cord 45
Near death experience 45
God Energy 46
The Universal Consciousness of God 47

Chpt. 6:   What does God do? 49

Chpt. 7:   Where do I find God? 53
Your Soul and your Higher Self 55
Accessing your Higher Self 56
Limited memory 57
What happens when you are sleeping? 60
Praying to God.. 62

Page

PART THREE: WHAT YOU NEED TO KNOW!

Chpt. 8: The meaning of love 65

Chpt. 9: We are all one 69

Chpt. 10: Your Aura 75
Protecting your Aura and your energy 79

Chpt. 11: Your Chakras 81

PART FOUR: OTHER REALITIES

Chpt. 12: 2012 and all that! 85
Higher dimensions and higher vibrations 88
Advanced and primitive civilisations 91

Chpt. 13: Angels and Archangels 98

Chpt. 14: Spirit Guides 105

Chpt. 15: The Elemental Kingdoms 107

Chpt. 16: Famous Nature Poets 113

Page

PART FIVE: PLAYING THE GAME!

Chpt. 17: The Game of Life 128

Playing by the rules 133
The Law of Giving and Receiving 134
The Law of Gratitude 138
The Law of Forgiveness 139
The Law of Karma 143

EPILOGUE: Life is but a game! Go with the flow! 145

ABOUT THE AUTHOR

Eileen McCourt is a graduate of University College Dublin with a Master's degree in History. She is a retired professional school teacher of History and English.

A Reiki Grand Master, she teaches the following to all levels:

- Traditional Tibetan Usui Reiki

- Rahanni Celestial Healing

- Magnified Healing of the God Most High of the Universe

- Fire Spirit Reiki (Christ Consciousness and Holy Spirit)

- Archangel Reiki

- Mother Mary Reiki

- Violet Flame Reiki

- Unicorn Reiki

- Pegasus Reiki

- Dolphin Reiki

- Elementals Reiki

- Dragon Crystal Reiki

- Golden Eagle Reiki (Native American)

- Lemurian Crystal Reiki

- Okuna Reiki (Atlantean and Lemurian)

- Goddess of Light Reiki
- Tera-Mai Reiki Seichem
- Psychic Surgery

Eileen is also a practitioner of Angelic Reiki; Golden Rainbow Ray Reiki; Golden Chalice Reiki.

She has qualified in Ireland, England and Spain: in England through the Lynda Bourne School of Enlightenment, West Midlands; in Spain through the Spanish Federation of Reiki with Alessandra Rossin, Bienestar, Santa Eulalia, Ibiza.

Eileen lives in Warrenpoint, County Down, Northern Ireland and has travelled extensively throughout the world.

'Life's but a Game! Go with the Flow!' is Eileen's fifth book in just over a year and is a Spiritual book for today's teenagers and young adults.

Her first book, 'Living the Magic' was published in December 2014.

Her second book, 'This Great Awakening' was published in September 2015.

Her third book, 'Spirit Calling! Are You Listening?' and her fourth book, ' Working with Spirit: A World of Healing' were both published in January 2016.

She is currently working on her sixth book, 'Young in Spirit: A Child's first Spiritual Book', and her seventh book, which covers the family of Jesus, Mary Magdalene, Joseph of Arimathea and the Druid connection with the early Christian church.

Eileen has also recorded several meditation cds, accompanied by her brother, pianist Pat McCourt:

'Celestial Healing'

'Celestial Presence'

'Chakra Cleansing, Energising and Balancing'

'Ethereal Spirit'

'Open the Door to Archangel Michael'

'Healing with Archangel Raphael'

The list of outlets for books and cds, together with information on workshops and courses for both practitioners and teachers is on Eileen's website:

www.celestialhealing8.co.uk

e-mail: mccourteileen@yahoo.co.uk

In Bangkok

ACKNOWLEDGEMENTS

I wish to express sincere appreciation to the following, without whom this book would not have materialised:

My publishers, Don Hale OBE and Dr. Steve Green whose patience never ceases to amaze me;

Bronagh, Emma and Sarah at Mourne Office Supplies, Warrenpoint, for all their work and unfailing support;

My family and friends, both here on the earth plane and those back in Spirit, who continue to guide me and watch over me from the Higher Realms;

Margaret Hurdman, who has always believed in me and who now continues to guide and inspire me from her higher vantage point, having just recently passed back to Spirit. We will miss you Margaret!

All those who have bought my books and cds and all who have attended my workshops and courses;

All who have written reviews for me;

Above all, thank you Spirit, for all the blessings and gifts you continue to shower on me each and every day.

I do hope that these books are helping someone, somewhere, to find peace and harmony in life and to understand the reason why we are all here on Planet Earth at this particular time.

We are truly blessed!

Eileen McCourt

26 February 2016

REVIEWS

"A most comprehensive book on Spiritual awakening for the young at heart. This book is written in an easy to understand way which will appeal to teenagers or Spiritual people new to the subject.

The author has used honest and soul searching words which will lead the reader along a Spiritual path to new beginnings. An informative and well worth read."

Lynda Bourne, School of Enlightenment, West Midlands.

"*I am delighted to write this review as I think books aimed at children, and particularly teenagers, are vital. In this very challenging world, children are being met with many questions and along comes this wonderful book to help them. Having had three children myself I can really see how beneficial this book will be in helping to answer some of those questions. Eileen, as a retired schoolteacher and with her vast Spiritual knowledge, is the perfect person to write such a book. It is a very easy read, yet it covers so much!*

Well done, Eileen! Another masterpiece!"

Janet Kingston, Angel Times, 26 Thomas Street, Limerick.

'Well! Another ground breaker for Eileen McCourt!! An honest, no-holds barred, 'no-dumbing down', view of Spirituality for a younger audience!! To engage a teenage audience on anything, other than 'Playstation' or 'The Kardashians', is no mean feat. Eileen goes a long way towards this, with great eloquence, by sticking to three simple rules: honesty, meaning and simplicity.

To be honest, to say that 'Life's but a Game' is a book for

teenagers or younger people, is limiting the scope of the book. This is a Universal book, a book that deals with Universal issues that affect every single one of us, teenager and adult alike. From her earlier volumes, we can see that McCourt does have a talent for 'calling it' and 'calling it' in a gloriously uncompromising way!! Spirituality and Spiritual direction for a world in moral and Spiritual decline is a message we all need to hear.

in the humble opinion of this reviewer, one of the great social maladies is that our communities no longer have the significant benefits of traditional 'Rites of Passage' into adulthood. This was always one of the positive aspects of ancient, tribal societies, where the obligations and expectations of the young person are addressed and clarified. These issues of life, role and forward direction are beautifully and unthreateningly realised from a Spiritual perspective in this book.

in many ways, this book deals with these traditional questions, by offering a route map for a Spiritual 'Rite of Passage'. 'Life's but a Game' asks the simple, real questions, such as: What is Spirituality? Why should we have it in our lives? And how does it fit in my life, in particular? For those beginning on their path, these are the questions that matter.

The real beauty of 'Life's but a game' lies in one huge, implicit question. That is, 'do you realise how marvellous and miraculous you are?' What a gift of a question that is, for those on the cusp of responsibility in this 'mad' world...or for anyone, come to that!! This is a truly uplifting and inspiring read, offering real life alternatives to the previous guilt, manipulation and punishment models of Spirituality. A wonderful and timely message!

Declan Guigley of Anam Nasca, Shamanic Practitioner, Author and Tutor. Declan lives in County Down, Ireland. To contact Declan, visit anamnasca.wordpress.com; Anam Nasca on Facebook; or drop him a line on anamnasca@gmail.com

FOREWORD

If you have this book in your hands, then it is for you. You have been drawn to it for a reason.

You are most probably a teenager or young adult. Or you could be a parent or guardian considering buying this book for a teenager or a young adult.

Our young people live in a messed-up world, a mess that they have had no part in creating.

There is confusion, frustration and bewilderment all around in the teenage ranks. Never before have teenagers been under so much pressure. So much is happening to them, all seemingly outside of their control. They are living in a bewildering world which they do not understand, and, indeed, a bewildering world that does not seem to understand them.

Teenage years are exciting times, or at least they should be! So much to do, so many places to go, so much to find out. And yes, so much fun to be had!

How sad then, that in this present world, so many of our wonderful, amazing teenagers are not having fun!

What has happened?

What has happened is that we have created a society that defines us by the amount of money we make, and the amount of material possessions we can accumulate. We have created a world where a fat wallet and an air-brushed, false image appear to count for more than a kind, caring nature. We have made our young people believe that life is all about money! We have placed our teenagers and young people in a no-win situation. We have put them under pressure to get a well paid career, despite the fact that so many are leaving our shores simply because there is no employment for them here! We have put our young people at risk of sacrificing their happiness and sense of inner fulfilment for a materialistic life style which cannot bring them either happiness or any sense of personal fulfilment.

There is pressure from parents, pressure from school, pressure to conform to what society expects of them, pressure from their peers, pressure to follow the crowd, to not be the odd one out, pressure from the beauty industry to have a certain look, pressure from the fashion industry to wear a certain type of clothes. They are bombarded daily by television, internet and media to conform to what others demand of them. And, of course, pressure from drug sellers, cigarette and alcohol companies, all promising them a quick fix to their problems.

That sure is a lot of pressure!

And all in those precious, fragile, vulnerable teenage years! Those precious, fragile, vulnerable teenage years where they are the target of so many unscrupulous sales and advertising experts who seek to exploit them for their own mercenary gains.

Left to their own devices, teenagers would not be in many of the difficult situations in which they now find themselves! Teenagers see everything in very simple terms; it is we who complicate everything for them! And we who have made such a mess of our own lives! We who have brought our world to the brink of destruction!

This book is an honest attempt to put things right, to bring balance into young people's lives again. To give our young people the knowledge that was denied us, the knowledge that will empower them to live their lives with confidence, happiness and fulfilment.

This book answers the questions which teenagers are asking, but which are not being answered. That's because they are not to be found in school text books or in teenage magazines.

Who am I? Where have I come from? Why am I here? Why is life so difficult? Why is this world so messed up?

And of course, the biggest questions of all!

Who is God? Does God exist? Where is God?

It is the answers to these vital questions that our teenagers and young adults are seeking! They need to be given the truth! They are entitled to be given the truth! That is the least we can do for them to make amends for what we have done to their world.

And, ironically, when they know the truth, they can change this world from a world of war, disharmony and inequality into a place of harmony, peace and love. A world where all people have enough, a world where all people are treated with respect, a world where everyone feels safe and valued.

If such a world is to come about, as indeed it can, it is going to be brought about by our young people. Who else can do it but only our young people?

And they can only bring about such a world if we provide them with the truth, if we provide them with the truth to the questions they are asking.

The truth comes to us all, each and every one of us, when and as we are ready. So if you have this book in your hand, you are ready for the truth!

And the importance of the truth is clearly emphasised in the *Gospel of Philip',* one of over fifty ancient documents found near the desert village of Nag Hammadi in Egypt, in 1945. This collection of texts, dating from the very beginning of the Christian era, is now having a profound influence on our understanding of the life and times of Jesus Christ. They are not part of what we call the canonical gospels, those gospels allegedly written later by Matthew, Mark, Luke and John. Rather, written by the disciples of Jesus and by Mary Magdalene, they offer us a different insight into the teachings of Jesus, the man known as 'Yeshua'.

The Gospel of Philip consists mainly of sayings and teachings of Yeshua. On Page 86, Plate 132, Philip writes:

"While hidden, truth is like ignorance: It keeps to itself. But when it is revealed, it is recognised and glorified, for it is more powerful than ignorance and error. It brings freedom. Ignorance is slavery, knowledge is freedom".

You are ready for the truth! You are ready for the truth that life is NOT meant to be taken too seriously. You are ready for the truth that life is meant to be fun, life is meant to be enjoyed, life is meant to be lived with enthusiasm and joy in every single moment. You are ready for the truth that life is but a game! A fun game!

And you are ready to learn the rules of this fun game of life! The rules that will guarantee you, without fail, to live a joyous, creative, fulfilling life!

It is no accident that you have this book in your hands right now at this moment, at this early stage in your life.

It is so important for you to learn the truth about life and about why you are here, right now, at this stage, at this age, and not at some time later. By learning all this now, by realising the truth right now, you are empowering yourself to have a wonderful future, a future where you can apply what you are about to learn about yourself, about this world in which you live, and indeed about other worlds, to bring you peace, understanding and tranquillity. When all around you may be losing their sense of peace and contentment, you will continue to live a life of joy and fulfilment.

You are indeed about to change our world! You are the future rulers of our world! You are the ones who will change all the systems in our world that have been so obviously proven not to work! You are the future makers of education policies, the future makers of economic policies, the future makers of monetary and fiscal policies. With the knowledge you gain in this book, you can take on these roles with confidence and assurance.

You can create a better world for everyone!

I send you love and light as you find the truth throughout these pages, and I send you peace and joy as you begin to see, understand and live your life as it is meant to be lived.

You will play the game of life!

The fun game of life!

And you will win!

NAMASTE!

Eileen McCourt

PART ONE: THE WONDER OF YOU!

CHAPTER 1

Who am I?

You are not just a physical body. Far from it!

You are actually two bodies. Besides your physical body, you are also a Spiritual body.

What is the difference between your physical body and your Spiritual body?

Your physical body

Your physical body is the body that enables you to experience life and to live life.

Your physical body is an amazing, wonderful, mind-boggling piece of machinery, much more so than any computer could ever be.

Your physical body runs, jumps, laughs, cries, talks, eats, thinks, feels, hears, sleeps and can do so much more. No computer can do what your physical body can do!

Your physical body has a heart, a brain, a liver, kidneys, lungs, intestines, bones, veins and all the other organs that all work together to keep you alive. No computer has anything like what your physical body has!

Computers can only do what someone else programmes them to do. Your physical body does not need someone else to programme it. Your own amazing brain programmes your physical body, constantly sending it messages, telling it what you want it to do. No computer has a brain like yours!

And your physical body can feel and experience all sorts of emotions; the highs, the lows, the fun, the happiness. A computer most definitely cannot do that!

Your five physical senses

You are able to experience life in your physical body through your five physical senses.

First, you can see all that is in front of you and around you with your eyes. All the people, the places, the animals; all the colours; the rainbows, the blue sky, the clouds; the sun, the moon and the stars.

Secondly, you can hear all the sounds around you with your ears. The birds singing, twittering and tweeting; the wind sighing in the trees; the leaves rustling on the ground in autumn; the rivers and streams gurgling as the water tumbles down over the stones; people laughing and talking; thunder roaring across the sky.

Thirdly, you can smell the different scents and aromas that are constantly wafting past your nose. The perfume from the flowers and trees; the refreshing aroma after a shower of rain; the tempting aroma of the dinner in the oven; the comforting scent of your pet; the fresh, sweet, earthy scent of your baby brother or sister just after their bath.

Fourthly, you can taste everything with your tongue and your mouth. The different flavours in your food; the salt water when you are in the sea; your own tears when you are crying.

Lastly, you can feel through touching things. The softness of your clothes; the lovely furry coat of your pet; the velvety feel of the grass or the gritty feel of the sand when you walk in your bare feet; the warmth of the soil; the softness of the flowers and trees; the wind blowing gently against your cheek; the warmth of the sun on your body; the coolness of the rain on your skin; the cold of the ice and snow biting at your fingers.

So as you can see, your five physical senses, in your physical body, enable you to experience the world as the wonderful place it really is. Life would be very dull indeed if you were not able to see, hear, smell, taste or touch! And these five physical senses all work together to support each other. For example, if someone is blind, then that person's sense of hearing or touch would be heightened in order to compensate for the lack of vision. It is the same with animals. The bat, for example, is blind, but it has extra sensory mechanisms to make up for that.

I am sure you can think of numerous other examples where someone does not have the use of all five physical senses, but is compensated for that in some way. The physical senses work together and support each other. That just shows what a truly amazing body you have!

So when you consider all that your physical body does for

you, then it is obvious that this physical body of yours needs looking after and nourishing. You need to dress your physical body in appropriate clothes in order to keep it warm or cool, depending on the weather. You need to feed your physical body the proper foods to keep it healthy and strong, to enable it to do all the things you want it to do for you. You need to exercise your physical body to keep it fit and healthy, so that it will be able to carry you around. And you need to allow your physical body to have sufficient sleep so that it will have enough energy to help you through your day.

As you grow older, your physical body changes into an adult body. You grow taller, you gain weight, and you now ask your physical body to do different things. And, of course, you still need to care for it!

The more love and care you give to your physical body, the longer it will be able to keep you alive. You might even live to be over one hundred years old!

Beyond your physical senses

However, there are some things your five physical senses cannot register. They are called your *physical* senses because they enable you to experience *physical* things, or what we call *physicality*. But there are other things besides physical things!

For example, every day you have numerous thoughts going through your head. You are always thinking! As a human being, that is what you do, constantly! You think! But, have you ever seen a thought? Ever heard a thought? Ever tasted a thought? Ever felt a thought? Ever smelt a thought? I don't think so!

Likewise, you are always having and expressing your opinions. But have you ever seen, heard, felt, tasted or smelt an opinion? I don't think so!

So you see, there are some things your physical body cannot register. In other words, your physical body is limited in the way it enables you to experience the world. Right?

So there must be some other sensory mechanisms that you have that enable you to experience beyond your five physical senses, such as thoughts or opinions. Right?

So there must be something else other than physical things, other than physicality. Right?

Let's now consider your other body, your Spiritual body.

Your Spiritual body

This Spiritual body of yours is called your soul.

This is the you that people cannot see. And why not?

People cannot see your Spiritual body simply because it is not *physical*. It has no *physicality*. And because it has no physicality, it cannot be monitored by any of your five physical senses.

Your soul cannot be seen or heard, tasted, felt or smelt by anyone else. No surgeon, during an operation, has ever found a soul floating around in a body! Nor has any surgeon ever seen a thought or an opinion floating about in there! Hardly!

You have just seen why you need to look after your physical body, and how you look after it. And just as you need to look after and care for your physical body, so too, you also need to look after and care for your Spiritual body, your soul. Even more so! And why?

You need to care for your soul even more than you care for your physical body because your soul, unlike your physical body, is immortal. That means that there will never be an end to your soul. It will go on for ever. When you no longer need your physical body, you will discard it, and it will die. Just like when you no longer need a particular item of clothing because you have outgrown it, so too, you will someday have no further need for your present physical body and you will leave it. That is when your physical body dies.

It is, however, only your physical body that dies. Your Spiritual body, your soul, is a very different matter!

Your soul has always been in existence, and always will be in existence for all eternity.

Your soul is what connects you to God, and so it is a bright shining Light. Your soul has come from God and is part of God. So you have Divine essence within your being. The essence of anything is what it is made from. So, as you are made from God, you are Divine essence. Your soul is Divine essence, a part of God.

When God created life, He did so by separating Himself into

countless smaller parts of Himself. Each one of these parts is a spark of God and is called a soul.

And that is who you are! You are one of these precious souls!

WOW!

This is another way of saying that you were made in the likeness of God. Your God essence shines out from you through a very bright light. You are the Light of God!

And acknowledging yourself as God essence is not some sort of Spiritual arrogance or big-headedness. It is just you accepting your real nature. It is just you accepting who you really are!

Feeding your Soul

You need to feed your soul in order to keep it bright and beautiful. And how do you feed your soul?

You feed your beautiful soul by doing things that make your soul happy. And the happier your soul is, then the more brightly and magnificently it will shine.

You make your soul happy by doing what you like doing and what you enjoy doing. If you like painting, then your soul is really happy when you are painting. If you like music, dancing, singing, writing, playing sports, making things, baking, pottering about in boats or in the garden, then your soul enjoys all the nourishment and food it gets from you doing just that. In other words, when you are happy and having fun, then your soul just loves it!

You feed your soul too, by being kind to other people, by sharing what you have with them, especially with those who do not have as much as you have. Your soul really loves it, too, when you are kind to animals; when you say good things about other people; when you refuse to carry gossip or stories about other people; when you refuse to join in with others to laugh or scoff at other people and when you defend others against bullies or those who are causing them hurt in any way.

Now you know!

So, you now know who you are!

You are a Spiritual being, a spark of Divine essence, having a physical experience in this life-time. You are a Spiritual being, being physical for a short period of time. You are occupying your present physical body only for this life-time. Your physical body is limited to what people see, because it is physical matter, whereas your soul, your Spiritual body, not being physical matter, has no limits. Your Spiritual body is immortal, it will never end, unlike your physical body which is only ever meant to be temporary.

CHAPTER 2

Where have I come from?

This is most probably not the first time you have been here on this earth. You have probably experienced many previous life-times here and you will probably experience many more life-times here.

Reincarnation

This process of returning for another life-time is what we call *'Reincarnation'*. We *'re-incarnate',* which means we come back again in the form of a physical body to live another life.

And why would we want to do that?

We want to do that simply because we want to experience life in all its many forms. And we cannot do that in just one life-time. We can only be one person at any one time! We cannot be two people at once!

So, where have you come from? Where were you before you were born into this present life-time? Where were you before you joined your mother in her womb?

First of all, remember what you have just read in the previous chapter about how God created you as a part of Himself? Well, that was a very long time ago! Countless millions and trillions of years ago. In fact, because you are actually a part of God, and God had no beginning, that means that you too, have been in existence since forever and ever.

So what have you been doing all this time? Where have you been? Where else were you besides in this life-time?

To answer this, first let me ask you another question!

Eternity

What do you think of when you think of eternity? Something that starts when you die and then goes on forever and ever without end?

NO! Eternity is NOT something that starts just after we die!

Eternity is right here and now. You are, right now, experiencing a part of eternity! You, right now, are actually in one phase of your long walk-about across eternity. You, right now, as a human being, are living through eternity!

Picture it all as a never-ending journey. A journey with adventure after adventure after adventure, forever and ever. And guess what! We get to choose the adventures we want to experience!

Cool or what!

So, each life we have is an adventure. This life you are now living is just one of the countless adventures you have already experienced and just one of the countless adventures you have yet to experience. Each and every one of these adventures is full of excitement and surprises, twists and turns. And in between each of these adventures, you return to the Spirit world, to where we call Heaven, where you start to plan your next adventure. How awesome is that!

Remember, your physical body is only for this one life-time, and when you no longer need it, it dies. But what about your other body? What about your Spiritual body? That body you call your soul? What happens to your soul when your physical body dies?

You know your soul does not die with your body, because your soul is immortal. So where does your soul go?

Your soul returns to where it came from, back to Heaven, back to the Spirit world. Back once again to the same place to where it returns after each and every life-time.

So now you know where you were just before you arrived in this life-time! You were in Heaven, and it was directly from Heaven that your soul arrived in your mother's womb.

And what exactly is your soul doing in Heaven in between life-times?

Besides continuing to enjoy all the things you enjoyed doing on earth, your soul is also planning its next adventure!

Your soul is planning for you to reincarnate yet again. Your soul is working out the reasons why you will come again to live in this world.

Now read on to find out why you are here!

CHAPTER 3
Why am I here?

Now that you know who you are and where you have come from, it is time to consider why you are here.

You are here for two main reasons.

First, as you learned in a previous chapter, you have been here many times before, and you will probably be here many more times again in order to experience all the different kinds of lives that it is possible for you to experience, but which you cannot experience in just one life-time.

However, there is another reason for you being here.

You are here in order to learn.

To learn what?

Remember what I told you about your physical body being only temporary while your Spiritual body, your soul, is immortal?

Well, your immortal soul is the other reason why you are here. In fact, your soul is '*thee*' reason why you are here. You are here in order to develop and evolve your own soul, to let your soul grow. You are here to raise your own Spiritual awareness, and the collective Spiritual awareness of all humanity. That means to help your soul become more aware of its Divine origins, and to help everyone else become more aware as well.

Your immortal soul is presently on its long walk-about across eternity, on a constant mission to grow and progress from soul infancy to soul maturity. And to do that, your soul needs to learn a lot of lessons.

Earth school

What has your soul wanting to learn lessons in order to grow, got to do with you being here on planet earth right now?

Well, when you are in Heaven, it is very difficult to learn lessons, because there is only love there. There is no such thing as war, hatred, selfishness, envy, spite, or any other of what we call *negative* feelings. These negative feelings are only found here on planet earth. They are *human* things. So souls in Heaven all desire to come to earth for another life in order to learn the lessons that they can only learn here on earth.

Think of earth as the best school for souls to learn lessons. And that is why you are here. To learn lessons! And with every lesson you learn, you collect brownie points.

And why is collecting brownie points '*soooooo*' important?

Collecting brownie points

Collecting brownie points is so important simply because, when you return to Heaven after each life-time, the more brownie points you have succeeded in collecting, then the greater the reward you will receive. So more lessons learned means more brownie points collected! And the more brownie points collected means the greater the reward. It's as simple as that!

And what lessons are you here to learn?

You are here to learn the lessons you yourself have decided you want to learn. And nobody can learn these lessons for you. Only you can learn your own lessons. You wouldn't expect anyone to learn a passage from Shakespeare for you, would you? That would be rather stupid! They can help you learn it, but they cannot learn it for you. Only you can do that. And equally, you cannot learn any lesson for anyone else. NO! We have all got to learn our own lessons! We have each got to live our own life! And we have each got to allow others to live theirs! Each of us is on our own path, chosen by us, nobody else.

So, you are here to learn. You are here to learn how to evolve your soul. You are here to learn how to make your soul happy. And remember how you make your soul happy?

You make your soul happy by doing what you love doing, and by spreading love, charity, kindness, caring, forgiveness, compassion, gratitude and tolerance to as many people as you can while you are here.

And the good news in all of this?

The good news in all of this is that what you give out to other people, you will get back ten-fold and more. And not just what you give out in your actions, but in your words and thoughts as well! When you are kind and caring towards other people, when you forgive other people, when you show compassion towards other people, it all comes back to you multiplied many times. Just like a boomerang! A game of boomerang! A friendly boomerang that you can catch!

But! How can you learn to forgive people unless there are people to forgive? How can you learn to be charitable unless there are people who need charity? How can you earn brownie points through helping people if nobody needs help? How can you learn compassion and tolerance unless there are people who annoy you?

The key to understanding the answers to all these questions lies in the fact that God has given you free will.

Free will

Free will means that you can freely choose to do or not to do anything. Free will means that you can choose to come back to earth for another life-time or to remain in Heaven.

And if you do choose to come back to earth for another life-time, then you can freely choose what lessons you wish to learn this time around!

Remember what you read about being in Heaven in between life-times? How you were planning your next life-time? Your next move? Your next exciting adventure?

Well, let's see what happens after you have decided to return to earth.

You have certain, definite lessons to learn. You yourself have decided that. There are brownie points to be collected! No messing about!

You have got to plan every detail of your new life! You have got to cover every eventuality! Absolutely nothing can be left to chance! You are really busy!

Planning your life

Think of it all like creating a play. You need to think up a plan and a story. You need to write the script, and you need to decide who will act each part in your stage production. This is your play. This is your production. This is your life.

Besides deciding what lessons you want to learn, you have also got to work out *how* you will learn them!

That means considering very carefully where you will need to live. What kind of a body will you need? For example, if you want your soul to learn and grow through experiencing life as a disabled person, then you have got to design a disabled body specifically for yourself. Likewise, if you want your soul to learn and grow through experiencing poverty, then you have got to be born in a very poor country or into a very poor family. If you want to have loads of money in order to help people by sharing your money with them, then you have got to be born into a very rich family or else have a body, brain and intellect that will enable you to make loads of money to help others.

Get the picture?

Now let's move on to the next stage.

So, you have decided what you want to learn, the type of body you need to design for yourself in order to learn that lesson, and where in the world you need to be born in order to be in the right place to learn that lesson. Right?

You are still not finished yet, though! Your plan is still far from complete!

Where, for example, are you going to find all those people you want to help? All those people to whom you want to show compassion and kindness? All those people you want to forgive? And for what is it that you need to forgive them?

This is where your friends come in!

While you are planning your new life, your friends, who are also in Heaven with you, freely choose to help you learn these lessons you want to learn. And guess what? They will earn brownie points for doing that! So everyone's a winner!

Now let's see how this will all work out to everyone's advantage!

One of your friends, let's say, volunteers to help you learn to be more charitable and to help those who do not have as much as you have. That friend and you might agree that he will live as a homeless person on the street. Another friend might offer to be a drug addict or an alcoholic. Yet another friend might volunteer to live as a murderer or a thief. And all just to help you! To help you learn certain lessons!

See what's happening here?

These friends of yours have sacrificed themselves to play out certain roles in your new life in order to help you learn the lessons you want to learn. And, of course, in return for that generous deed, they too gain brownie points, and you, next time, will help them to learn lessons in just the same way as they are helping you this time around.

So now you can see, if we can freely choose the kind of life we are going to have, then why would anyone choose to live a life of discomfort in the cold and misery of the street, rather than have a comfortable, easy life? There is always a reason for it! And a reason that we do not know about unless we were in on the plan!

And that is why we can never, ever judge anyone! Simply because we do not know who they are or what their story is. Simply because we do not know anyone else's plan! We only know our own!

Now let's go back to your plan, to you, and your friends who have freely and generously volunteered to help you.

That friend who is a homeless person living in the cold and misery, one day looks up and who does he see walking past him, ignoring his pleas for help? You, of course! It is you, the person with whom he made the agreement so many years ago! And what have you just done? You have just walked on past him, not even recognising him! You have just missed a super chance to learn the very lesson you came here to learn!

OOPS! There go those brownie points!

And your kind friend has to continue living in such misery in order to give you chance after chance after chance to learn that valuable lesson! That's some friend indeed!

Likewise, when people do what we call evil or cruel deeds, such as killing or hurting any other form of life, then what are these people doing?

These people, by being so cruel, are giving us a chance to learn a valuable lesson! But sometimes we don't see it that way! Often we tend to get angry with these people, and then what happens? What happens when we send out thoughts of anger and revenge?

OOPS! Here comes that boomerang again! Only this time, it's an angry boomerang!

OUCH! THAT HURT!

So what do you need to do? You need to learn the lesson that person is presenting to you! Those people are helping you to recognise cruelty and evil, and you need to show forgiveness and tolerance, even though they themselves have shown none. Remember! If you came here to learn the lesson of forgiveness, then you must have someone to forgive! Most probably that is one of your own friends who has agreed to act in that way in order to give you that chance!

Now consider this! As you choose everything that happens to you in your life-time, then you and you alone are responsible for all of that! There is absolutely no point in complaining or blaming God or feeling sorry for yourself, or playing the '*poor me*' syndrome!

And because you have planned all this in detail, there can be no such thing as chance or coincidence. Every situation and every person in your life enters and exits your life according to the script you yourself wrote! Every situation and every person has some message for you, some message to help you learn those lessons! You are the script writer of your own play. You are the director of your own play. And, of course, you are the main actor in your own play!

So, what must you do? How do you react to what you yourself have brought on yourself? How do you deal with the situations you yourself have created for you to experience?

You know the answer! Look for the lesson in all of this! And learn that lesson! Otherwise it will present itself to you again and again and again until you do learn it! And then, when you learn the lesson, what happens? You collect your brownie points! Well done!

All around us we see people collecting lots of brownie points. We see people going out in the cold and freezing nights to bring hot food and warm sleeping bags to the homeless people on the streets, chatting to them and just letting them know that someone cares about them. Why are these people sacrificing their own comforts to help others less fortunate?

Well, the answer might well lie in the fact that they too, at an earlier stage in their life, have experienced homelessness or living in hostels. And by experiencing this themselves, they are now in a position to show compassion to others in the same situation. They now want to help others who are suffering as they themselves have suffered. These people have learned the lesson that they decided they wanted to learn during this life-time. These people have got inspiration from their own situation as to how they can now help others.

I'm sure you remember someone at some time coming into your school to talk to all the students about some topical issue, like alcoholism or drug abuse? Well, did that person not tell you that he or she was at one stage an alcoholic or a drug addict? They have learned their lesson, and now they are helping others to avoid falling into the same trap.

So you see, every situation we find ourselves in has some very important lessons for us to learn. Whether we have abusive parents, alcoholic parents, or parents who neglect us or deprive us of love, or whatever other problem is in our family, then we ourselves chose to have that in our lives, so that we would then be able to understand and help other people who are experiencing the same problems. If there is a disability of any kind in our family, then we have chosen to be born into that situation in order to show love and to care for that person. We have just got to look for the lesson in absolutely everything that happens to us and in every person we meet.

That's the game of life! And that's how to play it!

Your parents

Now let us consider two very important people in your life. So important that you would not be here without them!

Your parents!

Like everyone else who comes into your life, you have had a big say in who your parents were going to be. In fact, you have actually chosen your parents! How awesome is that!

Your parents are your first teachers, and it is from them that you learn your early lessons. The lessons you have freely and specifically chosen to learn! So is it not perfectly obvious, therefore, that you will be very specific and definite when it comes to deciding about your parents? Nothing here can be left to chance!

You get to choose your own parents in one of two ways.

First, perhaps one of your friends in Heaven with you offers to play the role of your mother, and another the role of your father. Then, if they promise to help you learn the lessons you want to learn, and you agree to their offer, they leave Heaven before you in order to be old enough to be your parents when the time comes.

After they are born, you can watch them from your place in Heaven. You can see them grow up, and you might even arrange it that they meet and fall in love! How exciting is that!

As the time draws nearer for you to enter your mother's womb, you are really excited. You spend nine months in there, bonding with your chosen mother.

Then when you are born, you meet your new parents for the first time in this world. But remember, you knew them before, when you were all in Heaven together!

The other way you can choose your parents is when you don't want to wait that many years to come to earth. You are in a hurry and you want to come here as soon as possible! What happens next? There is not enough time for two of your friends to come to earth and grow up for about twenty years or more. No! You want to come here now! So what do you do?

From where you are in Heaven, you see everything and everybody. You look around and find who you would like to be your parents. You see the kind of people they are and how they are the best ones to help you learn the lessons you want to learn. Now you have got to get them together somehow!

You are going to play *'Cupid'!* That means, from your place in Heaven, you are going to arrange events that just somehow, will cause your mother and father to meet for the first time.

Then one day soon, your plans all fall into place! These two people meet and fall in love! And you have made it all happen!

Then, when the time is right, you join your mother in the womb and begin to grow into a human body, waiting for the time to be born. When your mother and father hold you for the first time, you feel their love and you smile, because you have a great secret! You bond with them immediately because, of course, you have played a big part in all of this!

And now you begin your new life with the parents you yourself have chosen!

Isn't that just awesome?

Learning the lessons

So you start to learn your lessons with your new parents.

You learn to show love to everyone and to planet earth. You

learn to help all those who are in need, like the poor, the sick, the homeless. You learn how to help your family and friends. You learn how to help those who are most vulnerable. That means those who are victims of other people's anger, spite or greed. If any of your friends are being bullied in school, for example, then you have got to stand up for them against the bullies. Bullies are just big cowards. They always pick on someone weaker or smaller than themselves, and never on someone stronger.

Every time you help someone, every time you share what you have with others, every time you make someone laugh, you collect more Spiritual brownie points. How easy is that!

And when you have completed your time here, the more brownie points you have collected, the greater the reward you will get in Heaven.

When you return to Heaven, you will not be asked what amount of money you made while you were here, what exams you managed to pass, or what possessions you managed to gather. There are no brownie points awarded for any of these! But you will be asked how you helped others and if you lived your life being true to yourself?

Being true to yourself

Being true to yourself? What does this mean?

Being true to yourself means doing what you enjoy doing, and enjoying what you are doing. And that means keeping your soul happy!

Being true to yourself means following your own natural talents and instincts, and not allowing anyone else to force you to follow their decisions for you, or convince you that they know what is best for you. Only you yourself knows what is best for you! Nobody knows you as well as you know yourself!

Being true to yourself means pleasing yourself, not in a selfish way, but in spending your life as you wish to spend it, because that is what you know you want, and not just to please others or keep others happy. For example, there is no point in taking on the family business just because others expect you to do so, even though you do not want to do that. Or choosing the same career as your parents, because that is what they want you to do.

No! It's all about YOU and what YOU want to do. You cannot live your life trying to please other people! If you are not doing what you love doing, and if you are not loving what you do, then you will not be happy. And if you are not happy, then you know how your poor soul will feel. Definitely not happy!

Being true to yourself means having fun and enjoying life, because that is what we are all meant to do. To have fun! To play! To laugh! To enjoy! Remember, life's but a game!

Being true to yourself means not allowing other people to lead you astray and do things you do not want to do or what you know deep down you should not do. Remember, you are made from God, so deep down, you know what is right, and when you choose to do the right thing, then you are being true to yourself. If you are not happy in any given situation, then you must get out of that situation. You must be true to yourself!

Being true to yourself means acknowledging your own feelings. Very often you might be told "*Big boys don't cry!*" or "*Don't be such a baby!*" But crying is natural for everybody, girls, boys, men, women, babies. We are all composed of both a feminine side and a masculine side, and we have to let our feelings express themselves in the way we want to express them, and not hold them in, just in order to please anyone else.

Being true to yourself means following your own instincts, accepting who you are and not going against your basic nature. Perhaps you are studying Shakespeare's '*Macbeth'* in school? Or perhaps you have already studied it?

Well, you know how Lady Macbeth went against her natural feminine nature in asking the powers of evil to make her as strong as any man in order to kill Duncan. How she asked for all of her feminine qualities to be removed so that she would not feel any remorse for what she was about to do. That was Lady Macbeth not being true to herself. That was Lady Macbeth not being the kind, gentle, caring person she should have naturally been, as a woman. That was Lady Macbeth denying her natural feminine qualities and instincts. She denied her natural feminine qualities, and look how that ended up! She went insane because she could no longer cope with the guilt for what she herself caused to happen. And all because she was not being true to herself.

When you go against your own natural instincts, living a lie, not being true to yourself, you are not doing anybody any favours, least of all yourself! And you know what will happen!

You will make yourself ill!

Perhaps you have studied Shakespeare's *'Hamlet'* in school? If so, then you might remember the very famous words of Polonius to Laertes: *"To thine own self be true, and it must follow as the night the day, thou canst not then be false to any man."* Remember those famous words?

These famous words simply mean that you must live your life being just you and nobody else. When you do something just to please another person or just to be part of the gang, then you are not being true to yourself. Don't worry about the gang. The gang will go away some day. The gang will not always be there. But you will always have to live with yourself. So if whatever you are doing does not please you, then do not do it.

Always look for the good reason to do anything. And if you cannot find a good reason, then be true to yourself and pass on that one!

You have been given free will, and you have a right to use that free will and make your own decisions about what you want to do with your own life. But, when you have free will, you also have a responsibility to use that free will for the good of everyone, and in the way that will not hurt or offend anyone.

So remember, you cannot live your life pleasing anyone else! It is your life. Everyone else has their own life and their own free will! Let them get on with it. And just you get on with yours! Be true to yourself!

And know that when you live your heartfelt truth, then you will fill your world with true magnificence!

Life review

When you return to Heaven after each life-time here, you look back over everything you did while you were here and see just how true you really were to yourself. This is what is called your *'life review'*.

During this life review, you will decide for yourself whether or not you learned the lessons you came here to learn. Every good action and every not so good action will replay out in front of you, and you will clearly see how you hurt or helped other people. Every time you hurt someone, by thought, word or action, you will now feel their pain, and equally, every time you made someone happy or helped someone, you will now feel how you made them feel.

Everything you do while here on earth is recorded in a great big Spiritual book called the Akashic Records. And guess what! You have a page in there with your name on it! And on that page, everything you have done will be recorded. And that will help you to decide what you are going to do next.

You might decide you did not learn the lessons properly and you would like to try again. Or you might be satisfied with how well you learned the lessons, and now you want to learn more lessons.

And you now know what happens!

The merry-go-round of life!

Here you go again! Here you go again on the merry-go-round of life!

You have a different plan; different lessons to learn; different adventures to experience; a different place to live; a different body, and of course, different parents. The same people might be with you, but they are all playing different parts this time around. Your father in your last life might now be your sister, for example.

It's all a game. And like all games, it is not to be taken too seriously. Like all games, it's not the winning that's important, but the taking part!

You are back again for another life on this earth!

Back again for another throw of the dice!

Back to play, yet again, the game of life!

PART TWO: THE WONDER OF GOD!

CHAPTER 4

We've got God all wrong!

We have all been brought up with a certain image of God in our head and we all believe we know who or what God is.

But what if I told you that image is wrong? What if I told you that image has been very distorted?

First of all, why do people distort things? To '*distort*' means to put a different meaning to something, to present it in a different image, to disguise it in some way. If you distort something, that means you are changing something in order to make someone else see from your perspective, probably because you want them to do something, you want them to behave in a certain way. What you are actually doing is, you are trying to control how they think! That means you are trying to '*manipulate*' them! But remember what I told you earlier about free will? You know we all have been given free will. That means we are free to do and think as we wish. When you try to manipulate someone's thinking, then you are interfering with their free will. Not good!

All down through history, various religions and institutions have distorted the image of God in order to control everybody.

But here is the good news!

The truth can only be kept hidden for so long! It will always come out in the end!

And that is what is happening in the world today. That is why there is so much confusion! The truth is emerging, and sometimes people find it very hard to give up or change what they have always believed in.

What God is NOT

So let's unravel what you have probably been led to believe about God!

First of all, God is NOT a big man with a long flowing beard sitting up in Heaven on his great big throne, weighing up souls on the scales and then deciding whether they go to hell, to be punished for all eternity, or stay with him in Heaven to sit on a fluffy cloud playing the harp, singing hymns and praising him forever and ever. Do you not think singing hymns forever and ever would soon become very boring? How could you possibly know that many hymns? I know I wouldn't! That means you would be singing the same ones over and over again! Forever and ever! How much more boring could it get?

Secondly, God is NOT a punishing God! At the same time as you have been taught that God is a punishing God, you have also been taught that God is all merciful and compassionate and, wait for it! FORGIVING! There is definitely a great contradiction in all that! God cannot be both punishing and all merciful and forgiving at the same time. Agree?

Thirdly, God is NOT dictating our life to us. Remember! God has given us all free will. And you now know how that all works! God does not interfere in any way whatsoever in our lives! You now know too about how the boomerang works! You now know that we must all use our free will responsibly, in a way that never hurts or causes suffering to any other form of life. The boomerang always comes back to us! And it is not sent from God! The boomerang simply returns to us what we ourselves send out!

Fourthly, God does NOT judge us! God does not judge us either in this life or when we die. Just as there is no punishment, so also there is no judgement. Remember what you have learned about your life review? How you yourself, when you return to Heaven after each life-time, look back over your life and you yourself decide how successful you were or how unsuccessful you were in learning the lessons you yourself chose to learn? And then how you yourself decide what you want to do next?

And there is NO final judgement either. Just think about it! Are all the millions and trillions upon trillions of souls supposed to reassemble for a final judgement, and then be sentenced to hell or rewarded by being let into Heaven? What happens to the souls who are already in hell? Do they get out for the final judgement? Could they now get into Heaven? Could there have been a mis-carriage of justice? But we were told that there is never any way out of hell! And what happens to all those souls already in Heaven? Do they have to come out again and face another judgement? Could they now be sent to hell?

So as you see, this image of God and hell has just been

made up and used to control people. But the truth always comes out in the end! In fact, Pope John Paul, in 1999 made a statement saying that hell as a place of fire and punishment does not actually exist.

Fifthly, God is NOT someone we can blame for how our life is going! You know now that with that free will of yours, you yourself have chosen what happens to you in each life-time! You know now that you have chosen every event in your life, every person in your life, even your parents, in order to learn certain lessons. And, of course, you yourself have even chosen those particular lessons which you want to learn! So there is absolutely no point whatsoever in blaming God for anything! We very often hear people ask why God does not interfere and sort out the mess this world is in, or how God allows this or that to happen. But WE have created the mess in the world right now. WE have created the mess with that free will of ours! WE have not been using our free will responsibly! God has had no part in all of this!

So, you see, most of us have indeed, got God all wrong!

But it's not your fault! The image of God as a frightening God has been presented to you by those who wish to control you. Those who try to control you by frightening you! Those who frighten you by telling lies! And you know what happens when you tell lies! You have got to keep on telling more lies, and then more! Eventually, you will trip yourself up and the truth will come out. The truth always comes out!

Do not be afraid! And do not be afraid of God! God is NOT that controlling, frightening, punishing person you have been taught to believe in! Do NOT let anyone frighten you about what or who God is! Do NOT let people frighten you by telling you that God loves you only so long as you obey him, and when you disobey him, then he punishes you. God will always love you, no matter what you do! End of!

So, if we have got God all wrong, then we need to find out who or what God really is!

We need to find the truth! We need to find the truth about God!

We ask the real God to please stand up!

Come with me now into the next chapter of this book to find the truth about what or who God really is!

CHAPTER 5

Who or what is God?

Now that we have considered what God is *NOT*, it is time to consider what God *IS*.

First we need to understand all about energy and how energy works.

We are all energy

Everything is energy. Absolutely everything. And that includes us. We are energy. Energy never dies. It just changes form. So too, we never die. We just change our energy form.

Remember you read about how you have always been in existence and how you will always be in existence, for ever and ever? How before you were born into this life you were in existence?

Well, you have always been in existence as some form of energy. You exist in this life too, as energy, only this time you have taken on the energy form of a physical body.

After you complete your life here on earth, you will, once again, return to Heaven and take on that brighter, higher energy that everyone has in Heaven.

All energy vibrates at a different level. The more Spiritually developed we become, the more Spiritually aware we become, then the higher our energy vibration becomes. Angels and saints are very highly developed Spiritually, so their energy vibration is really high, so high that we cannot even see it with our human eyes.

Everything we do sends out an energy vibration into space. So too, every word we speak. Even our thoughts send out energy vibrations.

Whatever kind of energy we send out attracts the same kind of energy back to us. Like attracts like! That's why you have the particular friends you have. Your energy matches their energy, and so they are drawn to you.

We must always be very careful about the kind of energy we send out in our actions, words and thoughts. You have often heard the phrase '*be careful what you wish for!*' And why? Because it will become real! It will attract to it the energy needed to make it real!

Perhaps you remember some time in your life trying to get off going to school by telling your mum you had a pain in your tummy or you had a sore head? You probably got away with it and you were allowed to stay off school. But I bet you that before that day had ended you really had a pain in your tummy or a sore head! Right? See what happened here? You sent out the energy that attracted the same thing back to you!

So too, if we send out negative energy, in the form of thoughts or words of envy or jealousy, hatred or unkindness of any sort, watch out! Your negative thoughts will attract the same sort of negativity back to you. It's that boomerang again!

On the other hand, when you send out kind, loving thoughts or words to everyone, then those kind loving words will come back to you again.

So always think before you speak about anyone! And always be careful about how you speak to anyone! Once that energy goes out from you, you cannot delete it or call it back and replace it! And you have to live with the good or the damage you have caused to happen!

Now consider this. When you leave home to go to school in the morning, how do you feel? Your feelings and thoughts, remember, create and send out energy! So if you are feeling all sad and annoyed, with a big scowl on your cross face because you have to go to school, then what sort of energy is that sending out? And what sort of energy will it attract back to you? You will get more annoyance and sadness, more scowls and more cross faces coming back to you all day, for as long as you stay in that mood. What a miserable day you will have! And you will have brought it all on yourself!

On the other hand, if you set off for school in the morning with a bright, enthusiastic smile on your face, thinking about all the wonderful, new, exciting things you are going to learn, then that is exactly what will happen to you! You will have an amazing, exciting, wonderful day!

However, the good news is that even if you do start off your day with scowls and a cross face, you are not doomed to the same for the rest of the day. And why not? Simply because you can always change your energy that you send out! It all depends on you! You are in control! You are in control of the energy you send out, and therefore, you are in control of the energy that comes back to you.

All energy attracts similar energy back to it! So whatever you want to have in your life, then you must send out the right energy in order to attract that to you!

That's part of the game of life! And now you know how to play it!

Energy is always moving and changing

Energy is not stagnant. That means it is always moving, always changing.

Your particular energy has drawn your friends into your life because the energy you are sending out is the same as their energy.

But what happens when your energy changes, as it does, constantly?

When your energy changes, you now send out your new energy and this might no longer be compatible with the energy of your friends. This is when you find new friends entering your life, as your former friends now exit your life.

This is all good news. It means you will always be spending your time with people whose energy matches yours.

Very often, though, it hurts for a while after friends leave you and are no longer your friends. Do not be angry or look for revenge on them! NO! You know where that will only get you! A slap with an angry boomerang!

Instead of being angry and cross with them, thank them for the lessons they have taught you. And they *have* taught you some lessons! That's why they were in your life in the first place! But you have now been successful in learning those lessons, so it is time for you to move on and allow other friends into your life, new friends who will help you learn new lessons. Just send your former friends love and thanks, and tell them, *"Thank you for being you!"*

Divorce and separation

Perhaps your parents are divorced? Perhaps you are living with one parent and you get to see your other parent as often as you like? Or perhaps you never see your other parent?

Again, let's look at what is happening here.

Remember how you chose these two particular people to be your parents? How you decided they would be the best parents to help you learn the lessons you want to learn? Well, that is true! You are learning from their situation.

But something else is happening here!

It's that energy again! That energy is changing again!

When your parents met and fell in love, that was because their energies matched perfectly. But as you now know, energy does not remain the same. It changes! Sometimes when two people love each other, they grow and change together, so their energies continue to match. And that is wonderful!

But very often, one person's energy changes faster than the other person's energy, and then they begin to drift apart. Their energies no longer match. And that is when all the shouting and angry words come out. Perhaps you have gone to bed at night listening to your parents arguing and fighting? Insulting each other? Maybe even being violent to one another? Maybe you have been afraid and scared? Perhaps even terrified?

Well, now you know what is happening. And now you can see that it is time for both your parents to let each other go and move on with their lives. And yes, it is very sad to see one of your parents leave.

But surely it must be better to see one parent leave than to have to continue to listen to all the arguments, all the fighting, all the hurting words? And you know how you have to deal with all this! Try and not feel angry or bitter towards them. You don't want that boomerang coming back at you! You have enough to deal with right now without that! Thank them for helping you learn the lessons, say "*Thank you for being you!*" and send them love. Be happy for them, that they are beginning a new phase in their lives, and know that they can be happy again!

You know the words of the famous song *'DIVORCE'?* Where the word is spelt out all the time, and never actually mentioned?

"Our little boy is four years old and quite a little man / So we spell out the words we don't want him to understand / I love you both and it will be pure H E double L for me / Oh, I wish that we could stop this D-I-V-O-R-C-E."

Remember that song?

Well, you now know why divorces and separations happen. It's all got to do with changing energy! Like everything else in life!

What happens when we die?

It's all about energy again! It's always about energy. It's always about how energy never dies, but only changes form.

So, when we die, we do not cease to exist.

We simply change energy form. Again!

We leave behind our physical body because we no longer need it and our soul, our Spiritual body, moves on as a different form of energy.

Now, remember reading about the importance of all those brownie points? Well, now it's time to produce them!

In Heaven, just as here on earth, there are different levels of achievement. Just as in school here on earth, where you move upward in different grades, so too, there are higher levels of achievement in Heaven. And the more brownie points you have managed to earn while here on earth, then the higher grade your soul will achieve in Heaven.

All the saints are very high in Heaven, simply because they have earned so many brownie points when they lived here on earth. So is Jesus. Jesus was a very highly advanced, very Spiritually evolved person while here on earth. That's how he could perform all the miracles and walk on the waters. Jesus is now in the highest level of Heaven. By being *'high in Heaven',* I mean that the further you progress, the lighter and higher your energy becomes. The most dense energy of all is here on planet earth, and that is why you have to take the form of a physical body here on earth. To match the dense energy here! Then, when you leave your body behind, your soul flies onward in its own much lighter, higher form of energy, back to the much lighter energy of Heaven.

So you see, Heaven is not a place as we understand a place to be. Heaven is not a planet or a star somewhere up in some galaxy. Heaven is not somewhere up above the clouds where God lives.

Heaven is an energy, a very high vibrational energy. In fact, Heaven is the name we give to the highest energy vibrational level of all. And just like all other vibrations of energy, Heaven is all around us.

Think of your radio. It transmits different stations and channels to you, all from different frequencies. When you are listening to one particular station, where are all the other stations? Away somewhere else?

No! they are still on wavelengths around your house. You are just not tuned into them. But they are still there!

Likewise, your television. When you are watching one particular channel, all the other channels are still on frequencies all around you. You are just not tuned into them! So you cannot see them!

It is exactly the same with Heaven and all other higher energy vibrations. Just because you cannot see them does not mean that they do not exist. It is not because they do not exist that you cannot see them. It is because they are on a higher energy vibration frequency, much higher than our dense earth vibration, where everything is physical matter. On these higher vibrational levels, everything is Spiritual, not physical.

Jesus said: "*There are many mansions in my Father's house.*" What Jesus meant by this is that there are numerous different levels of attainment in Heaven, and we progress up through the different levels according to the amount of brownie points we have achieved. Just like in school here, where we move up through the higher grades.

When your soul returns to Heaven, it automatically knows what level it has attained. And it can go to only that level. It cannot go to any higher level until it has achieved that level.

So, if you are on a lower level than your loved ones, does that mean you never get to see them?

Well, you know you cannot go up to their level, because you have not yet earned that level. So what happens? The good news is that they can lower their energy to meet yours. Remember, there are no physical bodies to move around in. Everything is bright, light energy. All it requires is a thought, and your loved ones are with you! You are all together now in this Spirit energy, a much lighter, higher form of energy than you were in when you were here on earth in bodily form. You meet all your pets again too, as they are also now part of this energy of Heaven.

So you see, it's always all about energy, and how energy

always changes and moves. Energy never dies. It just passes on to a different level. So no one ever dies.

Perhaps your grandparents have passed on to a different energy? Perhaps you were very close to them while they were here on earth? Or perhaps one of your parents has passed on to a different energy level? Or maybe even both of your parents are now in the higher energy vibration of Heaven?

Well you now know what this means!

It means they have not gone to a different place away up in the clouds somewhere. It means they have gone anywhere in fact! They are still around you, just like those television channels are all around you on different wavelengths. And you can tune into these higher vibration energies whenever you want! All it takes is a thought! All it takes is for you to think of your loved ones and they are with you. And they are looking after you still, from their vantage point of that higher energy frequency, where they are able to see the whole picture, unlike when they were here on earth, where their earthly vision was very limited.

So, after you spend some time in this higher energy vibration we call Heaven, you might decide you want to return to earth, to *reincarnate,* to have yet another go at playing the game of life. So you start to plan your next life!

Your next adventure! It's all so exciting! And you are in control!

The silver cord

Your soul is attached to your physical body through an energetic connection called the '*silver cord'.* This is similar to the umbilical cord that attaches the baby in the womb to its mother. And just as the umbilical cord feeds energy and nourishment from mother to baby, so too, this silver cord is the life-line through which your soul feeds energy and information into your physical body.

When the time comes for you to return to Heaven at the end of each life-time, your silver cord stretches as your soul exits your physical body, and then disconnects. This disconnection of your silver cord from your physical body is the point of no return for your soul.

Near death experience

A near death experience can occur when, for example, someone has been in a serious accident, or on an operating table, or maybe experiencing a heart attack and waiting for the ambulance to arrive. What happens here is that the soul is getting ready to leave the physical body. Then, just before the silver cord breaks, that person is revived again. So that person is still alive. The Soul has not left the physical body because the silver cord is still connected.

PHEW! That was a close call!

Most people who have had a near death experience all report seeing a great light in front of them and they are travelling towards that light. They are now a different form of energy, feeling weightless without their physical body. They are moving back into the lighter energy of Heaven. And it is all just so beautiful, calm and peaceful!

God energy

Now that you know that we are all energy, and now that you know and understand how energy works, let us consider all this in the context of who or what God is.

Have you guessed what is coming next?

Have you worked out for yourself that if you are energy, and you have come from God, then that must surely mean that even God is energy?

You are right! Absolutely right!

See how the dots all join up in the game of life?

Yes, God is energy. And in that huge energy mass that is God, is included everything and everybody that is, that ever has been and that ever will be. That is how powerful God is! God is everything and everybody.

Picture the sun in the sky. It is a great ball of light, spreading warmth and light across the entire earth, affecting everybody and everything. It gives life to everything through its rays.

Now picture God as a great huge white light, spreading over everything and everybody, not just on this earth, but over all the stars and planets in the other universes and in the entire cosmos. WOW! That's some light! That's some energy!

The Universal Consciousness of God

And that vast, unending God energy, that includes every thought that ever was and ever will be, and absolutely everything that ever was and ever will be, all the events in history since before time began, that knows all things past, present and yet to come, is what we call the '*Universal Consciousness of God.*'

And it is from this all-knowing, all-powerful Universal Consciousness of God that all life is constantly being created.

This Universal Consciousness of God is a vast stream of thoughts flowing through time and is made up of Spiritual, not physical matter.

And you are connected to this Universal Consciousness of God.

You cannot exist outside of this great Universal Consciousness of God.

Think of the different electrical appliances in your house and in your school. None of those can operate unless it is plugged into the electricity supply and unless it is turned on. Right? So too, you can have no life or no existence if you are not connected to the Universal Consciousness of God. And why not? Because the Universal Consciousness of God *is* all life and all creation.

So now you know that God is not a person.

Now you know that God is a consciousness, an energy, an all-encompassing, all-knowing consciousness and energy, out of which we have all emerged, and from which we have all been created. We are all part of God energy. We are all the same, but yet we are all different, we are all unique individuals.

Look at it this way. The wave is in the vast ocean. Just so, we are in God. Each wave is different. So too, each of us is different. The wave gets its life, its impetus from the sea. We get our life, our impetus, from God. The vast ocean is the support system, the support mechanism of the wave, the very giver of life to the wave. The wave can have no existence outside the ocean, because it is made from the very stuff of the ocean, the very essence of the ocean. So too, God is our support system, our support mechanism, the very giver of life to us. We can have no existence outside of God, because we are made from the very stuff of God, the very essence of God. If the wave could talk, when it is a wave, it would say "*Look at me, I'm a wave!*" Yet, when it retreats back into the ocean after every crash, after every life as a wave, it would say "*Look at me! I'm the ocean!*" The wave is both an individual, a unique wave, yet it is also part of the vast ocean. And that can never change. The wave can never, ever change its essence. And neither can we ever change our essence. We have always been, and always will be, part of the essence of God. And just as the wave has freedom to express itself in whatever way it wants to express itself, and come to fruition in its own way and time, so too, we have free will to express our God essence in whatever way we so choose. If the wave fails to reach its crest, the ocean does not judge, reprimand or punish the wave. The ocean does not say, "*You bad wave! You have failed yet again! You will be punished! You are no longer a wave! You must leave the ocean!"* So too, we are never expelled from the God essence, the God consciousness.

See the comparison between you and the wave? See the comparison between the ocean and God?

Now that you understand what God is, let us investigate further and see what God does!

CHAPTER 6
What does God do?

You have just read about how God can best be described and explained as energy. You have also just read about what God does *NOT* do. God does *NOT* punish. God does *NOT* judge. God does *NOT* dictate our lives.

So what, then *DOES* God do?

The answer is very simple and straightforward.

God creates!

That's it! The sum and total of what God does! God creates!

And God is constantly creating! God is in fact, the *'process of creating'*. God is the *'Supreme Being'*. That word *'being'* is not a noun in this case, but a verb. God is constantly *'being'* a creator.

God creates in order to experience all that can possibly be experienced. God experiences through everything that has ever been created and ever will be created. God experiences through us. So you are, in fact, absolute Divinity expressing and experiencing itself!

You know that energy is never stagnant. It is always moving, always changing. So too, God energy is always creating.

Look at it like this.

God creates us. Then God continues to create *through* us. God continues to create music, art, dance through us. God continues to create new technology, new methods of transport, all sorts of new devices through us. God continues to create new scientific and medical discoveries through us. This is our God Essence at work! This is God creating through our Soul! Remember what you read about who you are? How you are made from God? Well, that is how God can continue to create through you! God is in you! All the gifts each one of us is given are from God. That is God continuing to create!

And yes! Remember how you chose your own body for this life-time? That means you are your own creation! Right!

So that must mean that each one of us is a co-creator with God! Right again!

WOW! Cool or what?

So God creates in order for God to experience.

Now, if that is the case, then why would God create violence, wars and suffering? Why would God want to experience all of that?

The answer lies, yet again, in our free will. We are the ones who cause wars, violence and suffering. Not God! We can choose to use our free will in whatever way we like. But whatever we do, God is still experiencing that through us.

And it is necessary for us to experience opposites! For example, we cannot appreciate our good health until we become ill. We cannot appreciate the warm days of summer unless we also experience the cold, freezing days of winter. And we cannot understand and appreciate good unless we equally are exposed to the bad.

Remember, too, we are here to learn lessons, in order for our Souls to become more aware of everything about God. But if the world did not have any evil, if the world only had good, then there would be no point in coming here! There would be no lessons to learn!

So you see, God has created you in order for God to experience life through you. Everything you do, everything you say, everything you think, that is God experiencing through you! Even the way you shout and roar for your team at a football match; the way you tie your shoe-laces; the way you butter your toast; the way you clean your teeth; the way you fix your school tie; God is experiencing all this through you. And that is all God wants! To experience! And that is why God has created you! That is why God has created everything!

There is another thing God wants, however.

And what is that one other thing God wants?

The only other thing God wants from you is for you to enjoy and take pleasure in God's creation.

Look around you!

Look at Nature! God's magnificent, amazing, wonderful creation! The greatest show on earth! And yet, so many of us do not even notice!

Nature! The gem in all of creation! And we don't even notice!

How sad! Sad for God because we have failed to acknowledge such a wonderful gift, and sad for us because we are missing out on so much beauty around us, and all the lessons Nature can teach us.

OOPS! There go more brownie points!

CHAPTER 7

Where do I find God?

God is in everything and in everybody.

That means God is everywhere! There can be no place that God is not! There can be no person that God is not!

So you do not need to go into the church to find God. You don't need to go anywhere to find God. In fact, you don't need to look for God at all! And why not? Because God is everything and everybody and everywhere!

But most importantly, God is in you! You need to accept, first and foremost, that you yourself are made of Divine God Essence.

Then, secondly, you need to accept that everyone else is made of the same Divine Essence.

Every person is *'God made man'.* That means you are part of God, expressing God in your present form. But that does not mean that you are limiting God! Far from it! You are just one of the many vast, varied and unique forms that God takes. Human beings are not the only form carrying the God Essence within them!

No! God is in every flower, every blade of grass, every tree, every plant, every cloud, every rainbow, every star in the night sky, every planet rotating throughout the entire cosmos.

God is the whisper in the wind, the rustle in the trees, the warmth of the sun, the gurgle of the little stream as it tumbles over the stones, the rising and setting of the sun, the raindrops that fall from the sky, the snowflakes that meander gently down to earth.

God is the majesty in the soaring flight of the eagles, the nest-building instincts in the birds, the hunting skills in the lion, the innocence in the lambs and the deer, the wagging of the dog's tail, the purring of the cat, the smile on the baby's face, the roar of the crowd at a football match, the soft singing of a mother as she soothes her baby to sleep.

God's *beingness* is in absolutely everything. There is nothing that God is not. Nothing can be in existence outside of God.

God is indeed omniscient, which means having unlimited knowledge, knowing everything; omnipresent, which means being in all places at the same time; and omnipotent, which means having unlimited power.

You know what God does! God creates. God creates through us. We create our own experiences through our actions, our words, our thoughts. That is all God's creative power working through us. That is God expressing and experiencing God's own creativeness. Through all of God's creations, God experiences each and every aspect of God. And you are an aspect of God!

And what you are experiencing is what God is experiencing; what God is experiencing, is God experiencing the God self through you; God creating God, in the continual act of creating the God self.

See how important you are? You are a co-creator with God!

God is the collective experience of all of us!

So where do you find God?

Just look in the mirror!

Your soul and your Higher Self

Your soul and your Higher Self are your Spiritual body.

But what exactly is your soul? What is the difference between your soul and your Higher Self?

Your soul is the totality of everything you have ever been and ever will be.

Remember how you read that God divided the God energy up into countless parts in order to experience life? Remember reading that each one of those parts was called a soul? Remember reading that you are one of those souls?

Well, your soul, and not your physical body is who you really are. Your physical body is only for this life-time. But your soul is immortal, it will go on forever and ever.

Your soul includes your personality, everything about you, all your previous existences and all your future existences. Your soul is that part of you that is indestructible, as it is not a physical phenomenon. Instead, your soul is pure energy, pulsating and radiating throughout your entire physical body. And you know all about energy! Energy never dies. Energy just changes form.

When you re-incarnate into each life-time, you do not need to tale your whole soul with you. You take only a tiny portion of your soul with you, just the portion you will need for your earthly experience this time around, depending on your particular requirements each time.

What happens to the rest of your soul? The greater part of your soul that you are not taking with you?

This greater part of your soul remains in Heaven. This is what you call your 'Higher Self '. It is called your Higher Self, because it remains on a higher energy form than that part of you that is reincarnating, and which has to slow down its energy vibration in order to match the more dense energy of this earth plane.

Accessing your Higher Self

You can access your Higher self by *'going within'.*

What does *going within* mean? And how exactly do you *go within?*

You *go within* in moments of silence and quiet, away from the noise and turbulence of everyday living. You access your Higher Self through the peace and calm of the Nature Kingdoms. You access your Higher Self through the silence, just sitting quietly with yourself, acknowledging that you are a spark of the Divine, and seeing yourself surrounded by Divine White Light. Now ask your Higher Self, that part of you that knows all the answers to all the questions you could ever ask, what it would do in this particular circumstance. The answer you get back is coming from your own Higher Self. You can call it your gut instinct if you like, or your intuition. Just go with it! Trust! Follow your instincts! And why? Because they are Divinely guided! That's why! They are coming from your own magnificent, beautiful, Spiritual part of you!

That's how powerful you really are! The deepest source of wisdom and knowledge available to any human being is their own magnificent '*within'*, their own magnificent, shining Spiritual Light, within which are all the answers. That is you yourself tuning in to the limitless, unfathomable source of your own wisdom and knowledge, of your own Higher Self. You yourself are the power that created everything in your life, through your own pre-birth life-plan, and you will continue to do so. By *going within*, you take back your own power from those who would try to control and manipulate you for their own purposes.

You do not need anyone else to give you the answers! You have all the answers inside in your own being, in your own Higher Self! People need to get away from giving their power over to others who profess that they know best and that their way is the only way. If all people were to follow their own individual truths, with respect for each other's truths, then we would have Heaven on earth.

Limited memory

So, as you see, your Higher Self, that part of your soul that remains in Heaven, in the higher energy, knows absolutely everything there is to know. Remember, your Higher Self is

God Essence! Your Higher Self is the original, purest form of you, and so it knows absolutely everything!

On the other hand, that part of your soul that you have taken into this life with you has very limited memory and does not know everything there is to know.

And why has this part of your soul only got limited memory?

This part of your soul has only limited memory because it is for your highest good that it should have only limited memory.

Remember the reasons why you are here?

You are here to learn lessons! You are here to play the game of life!

And part of that game is about you finding the clues, joining up all the dots and completing the puzzle.

But if you knew all the answers to all the questions beforehand, then there would be no point whatsoever in coming here! The fun would be taken out of the game! The game of life would not be a game anymore!

Your Higher Self holds all the information you need for this life-time and also all the information you do not need for this life-time. And, of course, as you have just read, you always have access to your Higher Self.

But the problem is, your Higher Self cannot lie, so it just might tell you something that you do not need to know at this point in time! Your Higher Self might, in its innocence and total honesty just ruin the game for you!

So, for your own good, the small part of your soul that you take with you into each life-time here on earth, has only limited memory. The '*veil of forgetfulness*' has been pulled down over your eyes at birth to make sure that the life-plan you drew up so carefully before you came here is allowed to play out.

When you are born, you do not, however, immediately forget everything.

You have just arrived from Heaven. You can still remember some things about Heaven and your friends in Heaven. That's why little babies often look up at the ceiling laughing, as if they are seeing someone there. And they are! They are seeing their little friends and the Angels smiling down at them, laughing and playing just as they did when they were all together in Heaven!

For the first few years of your life, you might very well continue to be able to see your little friends and Angels, because your energy is still so pure and light, just like theirs, and you might continue to play with them.

Then, as you grow older, you begin to forget about all this, and what it was like in Heaven, because you have to concentrate on your new life here now in the present. And you find new friends to play with, as you start to learn the lessons you came here to learn.

You start to play the game of life! It's all fun! The lessons are all hidden and you have to search for all the clues!

And part of the game of life includes trying to remember everything you have forgotten! As you go through life and learn the lessons you chose to learn, you begin to remember those things which you had forgotten. Then the pieces of the jig-saw start to fit together. You can start to join up the dots!

What an exciting game! The game of life!

And you are now a player!

What happens when you are sleeping?

Sleep is a necessary and vital part of your life. In fact, you spend over one third of your life sleeping!

Let's go back to Shakespeare's character Macbeth again, and see how he explains sleep: *"Sleep that knits up the ravelled sleave of care / The death of each day's life, sore labour's bath / Balm of hurt minds, great nature's second course / Chief nourisher in life's feast."*

That's some list!

So, what actually happens when you sleep?

When you sleep, you dream. And your dreams are not just some form of in-house entertainment! Nor is sleep just a time of nourishment and rest for your physical body! Far from it!

You know by now that the sole(!) reason for you being here is to evolve your immortal soul. Everything is about your soul, and not your physical body. So sleep must therefore be very important for your soul. Right?

And it is!

When you sleep, your soul *'astral-travels'*.

That means that your soul leaves your physical body for a time and travels off somewhere on its own. And why would your soul want to travel off somewhere? And where does it go?

Remember, you only have a small portion of your entire soul with you here for each life-time. The greater part of your soul, your Higher Self remains on the higher energy level of Heaven. However, that part of your soul that is with you does not particularly enjoy being trapped inside a physical body. It is meant to fly freely! And that is exactly what it does when you are sleeping! So, when you are sleeping, your soul travels back to join the other greater part of itself in Heaven, to just enjoy being together with it, as One, and to enjoy, for a short while, the wonderful freedom of being without a physical body again. What a difference from the heavy, dense-energy physical body! A welcome release, indeed, from the earth plane, back to its normal, natural state!

And while your soul is in that higher energy, it gets nourishment, replenishment, reconnection and a re-energising. A sort of re-fuelling, really!

So, you see, your soul needs sleep even more than your physical body needs it! And you thought sleep was only for your physical body! In fact, it is your soul, and not your physical body, that decides when you sleep. It is your soul that needs a rest, and so it causes your physical body to fall asleep!

And the reason why babies sleep so much is simply because

they have just arrived from Heaven, and the soul finds this new experience of being in a physical body very difficult at first and very tiring. So it needs to re-fuel very often! Then, as the soul gets more used to its new situation, and begins to accept it more easily, it does not need as much re-fuelling. And so the baby sleeps less as it grows older.

Sleep is important for another reason too.

Remember I explained how, if someone you love has already passed on to another, higher form of energy. How they have not gone anywhere? How they are still all round you but on a higher energy frequency?

Well, it is when you are sleeping, when you are in that totally relaxed state, that they can most easily get through to you. They speak to you in your sleep, in your dreams, and give you messages. Perhaps you have wakened up feeling very certain that your loved one was with you? Well, that's because they were!

Sleep! What would we do without it? We certainly would not survive in this world!

Praying to God

You have been taught to pray since you were very young.

You have learned to rattle off words in various prayers, and sometimes, most probably, you did not even know what most of those words meant! And most probably, you are still rattling off the same words in the same prayers!

But have you ever considered what exactly you are doing when you are praying?

Well, let's consider that now!

When you are praying, you are probably thinking that you are praying to some outside force, some greater power out beyond you somewhere, who will, or maybe will not, grant your request. Right?

But that was *before* you read this book! That was *before* you learned the truth about God. That was *before* you learned that God is NOT an external force, but that God is *in* you, and that you are a part of God. That was *before* you learned that God is not a person with a form.

So let's now re-consider what praying really means.

You know now that your Higher Self is that Divine part of you, the part of you that is God. So, if you are praying to God, then you must be actually praying to your own Higher Self! Right? Absolutely right!

When you pray, you are actually asking your own Higher Self to give you the answer as to how you yourself can bring about the best outcome. Remember, your own Higher Self has all the answers! You are actually taking responsibility for your own actions.

So, when you pray to God, you are actually contacting your own Higher Self. And it is from your own Higher Self that you receive the answer in the form of guidance.

When you pray to the Angels and Saints, what are you

doing?

Let's now consider this one!

The Angels and Saints have form, unlike the God energy which is formless. The Saints have all been in life-times on this earth, so they have all had a physical body. Now, however, they are in existence as a much higher form of energy. Likewise the Angels exist on a much higher energy vibration that we do here on earth.

So when we pray to the Angels and Saints, what happens?

When we pray to the Angels and Saints, they do not make miracles
happen any more than praying to an external God does.

The Angels and Saints simply put us in touch with our own Higher Self. They clear the way to our Higher Self for us, making the connection easier.

Look at it all this way.

You arrive at the airport and discover that you have forgotten your passport. What do you do? Start praying? And hoping that the person to whom you are praying will suddenly make the passport miraculously appear in front of you?

Well, sorry to burst your bubble, but that's hardly going to happen!

It is your own Higher Self that is going to inspire you as to what is the best action you, and not God, can take to get your passport. So when you say a prayer to God, you are asking your Higher Self to advise you as to what you yourself need to do. You are taking responsibility for getting your passport. You are taking back your power!

So yes, continue to pray. But pray now like you have never prayed before! I'm sure you have often heard the saying: "*God helps those who help themselves*".

Well, now you know what that really means!

PART THREE:
WHAT YOU NEED TO KNOW!
CHAPTER 8
The meaning of Love

Poets, playwrights and writers have all written about love since time began, and they will continue to write about it. Literature is permeated with tales of love, and with stories about the romantic hero and even the romantic villain. So it must be of some significance!

In fact, it is of such major significance, that if we really understood what it actually means, then there would be no such thing as war, violence, hatred, jealousy or revenge.

That's a big claim!

So let's consider what love really means.

It certainly does NOT mean coming over all mushy and gooey, particularly on Saint Valentine's Day!

Firstly, love is unconditional. That means there are no conditions attached. If you say to someone that you will love them *if they do this or that,* or whatever, then that is not love. That is placing conditions on love. That is *conditional* love. That is manipulation. That is manipulating someone for your own ends. And manipulation is never good.

Unconditional love is the only kind of love there can ever be.

Unconditional love means accepting people as they are here and now, with no conditions attached. Unconditional love means seeing only the good in someone. Unconditional love means seeing the God Essence in every person. And because you see the God Essence in every person, then you do not judge, you do not criticise, you send out only pure thoughts of love and light.

Let me ask you a question!

If Jesus Christ, an Angel or any other Celestial being manifested in front of you right now, what would you do?

Would you rant and rage at it? Would you criticise it? Would you condemn it? Would you show hatred towards it? Would you try to kill it?

No! You would be completely in awe that such a wonderful, amazing being has come to you! You would bow down in respect and adoration! You would be overcome with humility, wonder and appreciation!

But that Celestial being is made of the same Divine Essence from which we are all created. And look at how we treat each other! We judge, we criticise, we condemn, we kill, we hate.

So what's all that about?

That is all about the fact that we do not see each other as the beautiful Spiritual being each and every one of us truly is! And if we could just start to see Divine Light in each other, then what a peaceful world we would be living in!

"Namaste" is a greeting in countries like Tibet and Bhutan. This greeting means "*The God in me recognises the God in you!*"

Just think about that! *The God in me recognises the God in you!*

What you are saying to someone when you greet them with the word '*Namaste!*' is that you see their God Essence. You see them as the bright, Spiritual being they really are, and as such, they are absolutely perfect in every way.

Now, if we could all manage to greet everyone with "*Namaste!*", and really mean it, then we would rid the world of war, violence and hatred!

WOW!

So now you see the power of love!

And you have that power! The power to change the world in which we live! The power to bring peace to all mankind!

The power of love!

Perhaps you know the words of the famous song, '*The power of Love'* recorded by Jennifer Rush in 1984? The song that topped the charts in so many countries right across the world?

"Don't need money, don't need fame / Don't need no credit card to ride this train / Tougher than diamonds and stronger than steel / You won't feel it until you feel / You feel the power, feel the power of love / That's the power, that's the power of love."

Or perhaps you know the words of that other famous song, '*All you need is love*', recorded by the Beetles in 1967?

"There's nothing you can do that can't be done / Nothing you can sing that can't be sung / Nothing you can say but you can learn how to play the game / It's easy / All you need is love / All you need is love / All you need is love / Love is all you need."

So don't forget, what makes the world go round?

Love! Of course! And you now know what love really means!

CHAPTER 9

We are all One

We have all been created from the same God Energy.

That means we are all made from the same *stuff.*

So therefore we are all the same.

And that God Energy includes absolutely every form of life that you can imagine in all the worlds and planets and stars that exist everywhere.

So, if we are all included in this great God Energy, that means we are all One. We are all connected. We are all one great big family in God! We are all the same energy, but just compressed in different and various ways to create different forms and different matter.

Now consider this. If we are all One, as you have seen we are, then, if you hurt anyone else, what are you really doing?

You are really hurting yourself!

So that is a really good reason to not hurt or be unkind to anyone else! Because you are really doing it to yourself!

And why would you ever hurt or be unkind to yourself? How stupid would that be?

Likewise, if someone attacks you, then that person is really a wounded, hurting part of yourself. And there is absolutely no point in giving back the same. Can you see why? Because you are only hurting yourself even more! You need to send love and compassion to that part of you that is hurting, and not anger or revenge.

And, of course, all forms of life, in all the eco-systems, are closely inter-related.

Take the trees, for example. They absorb our stale air that we breathe out, and change it all into oxygen which we then breathe in again. So part of the trees are in you and part of you is in the trees.

The food you eat has come from the soil of the earth. The sun has made this food grow by shining its warming rays on it. So when you eat that food, you are absorbing part of the sun and part of the earth. So the earth and the sun are in you.

Likewise, every rock, every mountain, every tree, every leaf, every river, every ocean is a part of us. And, of course, you and I are part of each other!

Get the picture?

We are all part of, and deeply connected to everything else in our own world and to everything else in the entire cosmos.

It's just all the various forms of energy constantly changing!

And even the tiniest little ant has an important job to do in this whole Oneness. That tiny little ant absorbs germs. The worms in the soil feed the birds. As do the berries on the trees. And look at the joy the birds give to us in their bird-song!

And, of course, we all need each other!

Think of all the people who are part of your life every day!

Your parents, your brothers and sisters, your aunts and uncles, your grand-parents, your cousins, your friends, your teachers. You need all of them!

Think now of all the people who are involved in keeping you alive!

All the doctors, the nurses and all the other people who work in hospitals!

All the people who are involved in getting food to you!

The farmers who grow the crops, the lorry drivers, who bring all the food to the shops all over the world, the people who make the lorries, the people who build the roads for the lorries to travel on, the builders who build the service stations where the drivers get petrol, the people who drill the petrol out of the earth and bring the petrol to the service stations, the people who pack up the shelves in the supermarkets where you can buy all the food!

Think of all the other people who help you!

The pilots and crews of all the planes in the world, the captains and crews of all the ships in the world, the people who make all the planes and ships, trains and buses, all of which allow us all to travel around this beautiful planet of ours.

Think of all the people who keep us safe!

All the people who collect our rubbish! They all do such a great job in keeping us safe from plagues and diseases that would happen if the rubbish was not collected! Perhaps your father works at collecting rubbish? If he does, then he is a real hero! You should be really proud of him!

All the people who clean our streets and public toilets! They are all heroes as well because they help keep all the rest of us free from germs.

What about all the firemen and ambulance drivers, all the rescue crews who go out in all kinds of weather to rescue people in trouble? Each one of them is a great hero too!

So you see, we all need each other. We are all connected. We are all One.

We are all held together by the most magnificent, the most awesome system of geometrical design amd mathematical equations, all supporting each other and needing each other.

The indisputable fact that we are all One is not something new in today's world. Sages, yogis and Spiritual leaders have been teaching this right down through history. Jesus Christ himself taught us about this Oneness over 2,000 years ago. So it certainly is not something new!

Mary Magdalene was a disciple of Jesus when he walked on this earth. She has been given a very unfavourable press right down through history, and has not been credited with the publicity and merit she truly deserves. Being very highly aware Spiritually, and being on a very high vibrational level, she understood more than any of the other disciples, the teachings of Jesus, and of them all, it was Mary Magdalene who was the closest to Christ throughout his ministry. If you look at the famous painting of '*The Last Supper*' by Leonardo da Vinci, you will see Mary Magdalene seated at Christ's right hand side.

The '*Gospel of Mary Magdalene*' came to light first in 1896 in Cairo, some fifty years before the momentous discovery of the collection of over fifty documents, hidden in deep secret caves near the desert village of Nag Hammadi in Egypt, in 1947. These revolutionary discoveries, dating from the very earliest Christian times, have been unearthed now, when a great awakening is taking place all over the earth plane, synchronised with the ending of a 26,000 year cycle and a 260,000 year cosmic cycle. No coincidence or accident! Remember, there is no such thing as an accident or a coincidence! All is synchronised to materialise in Divine timing. And the time for all these writings to emerge, writings hidden for over 2,000 years is now! These writings are giving us a very different view of the life of Jesus and his disciples than we have been led to believe down through history! The truth is emerging right now!

In her writings, Mary Magdalene clearly shares the teachings of Christ with us. Pages one to six of The Gospel of Mary Magdalene are missing, but the first piece of writing we get starts with a question to Jesus by Mary Magdalene, followed by Christ's answer: "*What is matter? Will it last forever?*" Jesus replied: " *All that is born, all that is created, all the elements of nature are interwoven and united with each other.*"

This is a simple statement from Christ himself, reported by Mary Magdalene, telling us that all things are interdependent and interlinked in the great vast complexity of creation.

Nothing exists in itself, by itself, or for itself. We are all connected and we are all composed of the same matter.

This is exactly what Spiritual writers, teachers and sages have been telling us down through history, and are still telling us today, that *we are all One.*

If we could just open our eyes and see that we are all One, then we would never hurt or injure another form of life.

All children would be safe. All animals would be safe. What a wonderful world it would be!

CHAPTER 10

Your Aura

You know now that all living things, including our physical bodies are filled with energy. This energy is just like electricity and it radiates outwards from our physical body.

This magnetic field that surrounds your physical body is called your '*Aura*'. It is oval in shape. That means it is in the shape of an egg. Everyone has an aura around their physical body. So too does every other form of life, for example animals, trees, flowers, mountains, rivers. If we did not have this aura around us, then we would not exist.

Some people can see the aura of others very clearly. Auras are very colourful and shimmering. They are always moving, like all energy, and can tell many things about us. A Russian man, named Semyon Kirlian has developed a special camera which can take pictures of the auras of people and all living things. This is called '*Kirlinian Photography*'. If you ever go to Spiritual or holistic fairs around the country, there is usually someone there who can photograph your aura for you.

Your aura tells you two main things. Firstly, it tells how healthy your physical body is and secondly, it tells how Spiritually developed you are.

Your aura is like a barometer for your physical body. That means it reflects how you feel. If you are sad and not feeling happy, then your aura will not be bright, but cloudy. You weaken your aura by negative thoughts and habits. For example, by not taking enough exercise, by not eating healthily, by not getting enough fresh air. You do your aura damage also by smoking, by alcohol, drugs or by getting insufficient sleep.

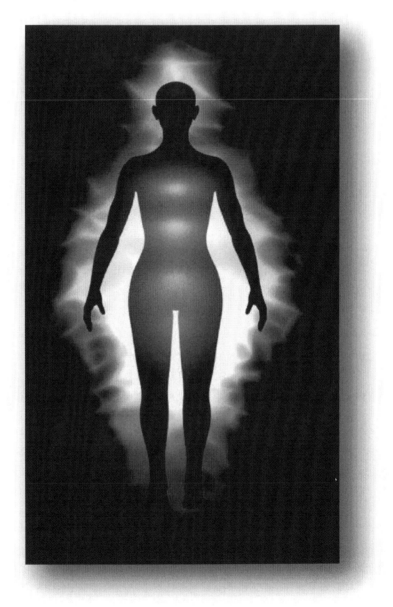

On the other hand, if you are feeling happy and full of energy, then your aura will be shining out very brightly. If your soul is happy, then your aura will be sparkling!

And you now know how to make your soul happy!

Your aura changes all the time. Remember, your aura is energy, and because energy changes all the time, then so too, your aura is constantly changing.

Every thought, every feeling you have, goes out through your aura. Notice how, when you meet someone, you either connect with them in a positive way, or you cannot get away from them quickly enough. Some people give you a lift while others drag you down.

This is all about your aura inter-connecting with the auras of others.

Perhaps you have noticed that when you buy new clothes, they feel strange when you first wear them? Have you ever wondered why this really is? This is because those new clothes have not got your aura, your energy, in them yet, until you wear them for a while, and then you become more used to them, as your aura settles into them.

It's the same thing with young children or babies. They usually have a favourite sheet or blanket that they just won't let go of, not even to get it washed! That's because they can feel their own aura in that sheet or blanket, and it gives them comfort. The child recognises its own energy!

Every flower, every tree, every rock, every mountain, every living thing has its own energy, and its own auric field.

Have you ever hugged a tree? Why not? Because you think that's stupid? Because you think your friends will laugh at you?

But that was *before* you learned about auras. That was *before* you learned about auras being a sort of personal barometer. That was *before* you learned that every living thing has an aura.

Now that you know all this, just go and hug a tree! What do you feel? Can you feel the energy coming from the tree? Can you feel the tree making you much more calm, much more peaceful? Now see what your friends are missing? Those friends you thought would laugh at you? Maybe they could do with a great big hug from a tree!

So next time you walk past a tree, send it love, hug it, and you'll be surprised how you will feel!

When you are happy and having fun, your aura will shine so brightly, it will attract the auras of other people.

However, your happy aura will not just attract other happy auras, but also other not-so-happy auras! These not-so-happy auras see your bright aura and try to get near it to get some of your aura's beautiful, bright energy.

We call these people *'Energy Vampires'!*

You need to protect yourself from energy vampires, because they will drain all your energy from your beautiful aura, getting their 'fix' from you, but leaving you feeling very tired.

Energy vampires also come in the form of computers, mobile

phones, televisions or micro-wave ovens. All that electro-magnetic energy sucks your energy, leaving you feeling drained and tired.

Protecting your aura and your energy

You always need to protect yourself against other people who drain your energy. These include nasty people who criticise you, complain about you, put you down, spread stories and lies about you, or who are jealous of you.

The energy these people send out is what we call *negative energy*.

And, unfortunately, it's all coming in your direction!

You need to protect yourself against this negative energy so that it will not harm you in any way!

And how exactly do you protect yourself?

You protect yourself by always having your shield up.

Your shield is the bright White Light of the Holy Spirit.

All you have to do is picture this bright White Light surrounding your whole body. Picture this White Light surrounding all your family, your friends, and anyone else you want to protect. If you have a friend going through an unhappy time right now, for some reason or other, then you can draw the White Light, in your mind, around them too, and you know they are protected.

You can also draw this White Light around your house, your car, your school, so that you will all be protected in all these places.

Another way you can protect yourself is by asking Archangel Michael to cover you with his Blue Cloak. Archangel Michael's job is to protect people and give them strength, but he can only help if you ask him to help you. This is because you have free will. So it is up to you to ask. Once you ask for help, Archangel Michael will respond immediately.

So now you are doubly protected! With the White Light of Holy Spirit and the Blue Cloak of Archangel Michael, you are safe!

But remember, you must continue to protect yourself every morning before you leave for school or for work.

You must always have your shield up! Your shield will keep you safe!

CHAPTER 11

CHAKRAS

In just the same way as your physical body has five physical senses, so too, your Spiritual body has seven chakras.

Your seven chakras are all different colours.

A rainbow has seven colours. And guess what? Your seven chakras are the same colours as the rainbow!

How cool is that?

And yes! No doubt you have already guessed! It's all about energy again! It's always about energy!

Your chakras are the energy centres of your Spiritual body, that connect you to all higher forms of energy and higher vibrations.

Remember what I told you about higher forms of energy and higher vibrations?

Remember what I told you about everyone and everything being energy?

And remember how I explained that the more Spiritually developed you are, then the higher your energy and your energy vibration will be?

That's why Angels and Saints are at a very high energy level! Because they are very advanced Spiritually.

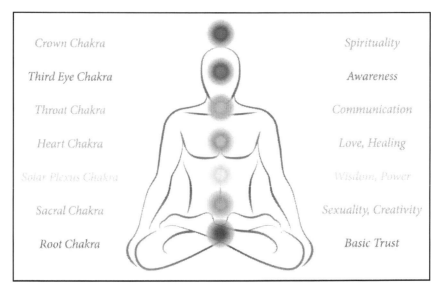

The seven chakras

We all develop Spiritually when we learn more and more of the lessons we are meant to learn. Every time we learn another lesson, we move up to a higher energy vibration.

Your chakras are like wheels, spinning round all the time, creating energy which then circulates around your body. All your chakras need to spin at the same rate, and when they do, then that shows that you are healthy.

Your first chakra is at the bottom of your spine. This is called your *Root Chakra*, and it is red in colour. When this chakra is spinning as it should spin, then you feel healthy, comfortable, safe and secure. You feel grounded, which means your head is not away up in the clouds! You have your two feet firmly on the ground! That means you are very sensible and not flighty! When this chakra is not spinning as it should spin, you feel as if you are all over the place. You can't concentrate and you are very restless. You are not grounded.

Your second chakra is called your *Sacral Chakra* and is just below your waist. When this chakra is spinning as it should, you feel very excited and enthusiastic about everything you do, and you are very creative. When this chakra is not spinning as it should, you feel bored, you feel lifeless, you just can't be bothered to make any effort. This chakra is orange in colour.

Your third chakra is your *Solar Plexus,* just above your waist. This chakra is yellow in colour. When this chakra is spinning as it should, then you feel very confident in yourself, very sensible and very enthusiastic. When this chakra is not spinning as it should, then you feel very low in confidence, unsure of yourself and uncertain how to behave.

Your fourth chakra is called your *Heart Chakra,* just where your heart is. This chakra is green and pink. Pink is the colour of love! When this chakra is spinning as it should, you feel very peaceful, self-loving, caring, compassionate and kind. When this chakra is not spinning as it should, you feel very critical, lonely, withdrawn and anti-social.

Your fifth chakra is your *Throat Chakra,* just at your throat, and this chakra is blue. When this chakra is spinning as it should, you feel you can communicate well with other people, and you are not afraid to voice your opinions. When this chakra is not spinning as it should, then you feel very shy, you feel you can't express your feelings or talk to anyone.

Your sixth chakra is right in the middle of your forehead and is called your *Third Eye.* This chakra is indigo in colour. When this chakra is spinning as it should, you feel very intuitive. That means you can see very deeply into things, you have very strong instincts and you can really see what is going on. When this chakra is not spinning as it should, then you feel very lacking in imagination, and you don't really see what is going on around you.

Your seventh chakra, your *Crown Chakra,* is right at the top of your head. This chakra is violet in colour. When this chakra is spinning as it should, you feel very connected to higher vibrations and very wise. You are very curious and inquisitive about God and why we are all here on this earth. When this chakra is not spinning as it should, you feel very confused, you are not curious about God, and you are very attached to material possessions. They are more important to you than being kind to other people, or making other people happy. If you have a baby brother or sister, you can see a little circle right at the top of their head. This is their Crown Chakra. The Crown Chakra can be seen more easily on a baby's head that on an adult's head because babies of course have only a little bit of hair or even maybe no hair at all yet!

Now, everyone your age has a very vivid imagination! Another word for imagination is visualisation.

You can imagine or visualise all your seven chakras spinning at the same time.

Just sit very quietly with your eyes closed, away from all the noise. All you have to do is see, in your mind, all your chakras, from the Root Chakra up to your Crown Chakra, all spinning at the same rate, in all their different colours.

You might find it difficult at first, but as you practise more often it will soon become very easy.

And then you will have a very healthy Spiritual body!

PART FOUR

OTHER REALITIES

CHAPTER 12

2012 and all that!

We are living in amazing times!

You have chosen to come back to planet earth at this time because you want to help in this *'Great Awakening'* we are all going through right now.

What do we mean by this *'Great Awakening'*?

By this *'Great Awakening'* we mean that people all over the world are *awakening* to the understanding of the nature of God, to an understanding of who they really are and to an understanding of why they are here. Many more people across the entire world are starting to realise and to accept that we are all One with God; that there is no such thing as separateness; we are all One, we are all connected with every other form of life on this planet and throughout the entire cosmos. That means that whatever happens anywhere in the cosmos affects each and every other part of the cosmos.

And the year 2012 marked a very big event in the history of this entire cosmos!

In 2012, two great time cycles came to an end. Firstly, a 26,000 year cosmic cycle came to an end, and secondly, a 260,000 year cosmic cycle came to an end.

What happened when these two great time cycles came to an end at the same time?

Something happened that had never happened before!

So what exactly happened in 2012?

In December 2012, the earth and all the other planets became as one. All their different energies merged into one, and the earth benefited greatly!

Earth's denser energy was raised to a higher vibration by the re-alignment of all the planets, with the result that we here on earth can now tune into the higher energy vibrations of other planets and universes all around us in space, much more easily than we could ever do before!

The veils between worlds and between different dimensions and energy vibrations are thinning. That means that it is much easier for us here in our more dense earth vibration to make contact with higher forms of energy, and for those higher forms of energy to make contact with us, if they so wish.

How is this good for planet earth and for us?

Well, as usual the explanation lies in understanding energy and how energy works! Remember, it's always about energy!

And you know how energy works! You know how everything is energy and how energy is always changing.

Energy works on different levels. We call these different levels '*vibrations*'. As your soul develops and evolves, then you move up through the higher levels of energy. That means you are on a higher, faster vibration, where your energy is more pure and much lighter. Each time you decide to reincarnate on planet earth, you have to slow down your energy vibration to match the more dense energy vibration here.

Each time you decide to reincarnate here on planet earth, you have to descend down through the various higher energy levels. This coming down to the earth energy is what we call coming down the '*vibrational corridor*'. When we say '*coming down*' we do not actually physically come down from the clouds somewhere. Because remember! These higher vibration energy levels are not places as we know places to be. They are just like higher forms of Spiritual awareness, all around us, but just not in physical form. Just like all the different radio or television channel frequencies all around us.

So coming down the vibrational corridor simply means you are *slowing down* your energy high vibrational rate to adapt to the much slower earth energy. So much slower, in fact, that it requires a physical body to live here!

Higher dimensions and higher vibrations

Our planet earth is not the only planet in the entire galaxy or the entire cosmos. Far from it!

We are surrounded by countless planets and stars, above, below and all around us.

Our planet earth is unique, however, in that we need certain things in order to be able to live here.

Firstly, we need oxygen; we need to breathe. Secondly, we also need food; we need to eat.

And of course, we need gravity! We need to stay firmly on the earth! Otherwise we would all be floating around in space somewhere!

So, like everything else in the Divine Grand Design, our bodies are equipped and designed with what is necessary to live in this world, in this earth energy vibration.

All the other planets and stars have life on them too. But it is not life as we know life to be here on planet earth. That's because it does not need to be!

The life on each and every planet is different, depending on the conditions on each planet.

But life is not just to be found on different physical planets and stars.

Life is also to be found on different dimensions and energy vibrations.

Remember what you learned about physical matter and physicality? How your physical body and your Spiritual bodies differ? How your physical body can be seen by others because it is physical, whereas your Spiritual body, your soul, cannot be seen?

Remember too, you learned that you are on a mission here for your soul to grow and develop, and as it does that, then it progresses up through the higher forms of energy, up through the higher dimensions and vibrations? This is what we call the *'cosmic elevator'*. Just like the *'vibrational corridor',* except in reverse!

There is life on all these different vibrations. Life, though, not as we know it. There are no physical bodies like ours, because bodies like ours are not needed.

All these higher dimensions and energy vibrational levels exist all around us. And again, they are constantly moving. Constantly moving along what we call the *'vibrational highway'.*

Many people now, as a result of what happened in 2012, can see forms of energy swirling around. Perhaps you can see energy swirling around in your bedroom at night? Many more people than ever before can also now see angels. Again that's because of the thinning of the veils between the different levels.

Perhaps you can see angels? Perhaps you have been told not to say anything about it? Perhaps you have been scolded by your parents for saying such things? Or perhaps you have learned to say nothing, to keep quiet about such things for fear of being laughed at or scolded? Or perhaps you thought you were going mad?

Well, the good news is, you are NOT going mad!

And the even better news?

The even better news is that you ARE seeing angels and possibly other Heavenly beings as well!

And why and how are you seeing these when your parents or friends are not seeing them?

Well, you are able to see these beings from other dimensions and vibrations simply because your own energy vibration is actually less dense than the energy vibration of the rest of us here on planet earth. You are very special indeed! You are so strongly connected to the whole God energy that these higher vibrational energy levels can contact you! So feel yourself very privileged indeed! These beings are your friends! Talk to them as you would talk to your friends!

Remember, though, what you learned about protecting your energy! If you are seeing Angels and other higher beings of Light, then you certainly need a lot of protection! And why? To protect you from mischief makers who might also want to contact you! You do not want any of these in your life!

So remember to always have your shield up! Your shield of the White Light of Holy Spirit and the blue cloak of Archangel Michael. Archangel Michael will always protect you, but remember, you have to ask!

Ask Archangel Michael to always be with you in every situation. Then you can happily talk to your angel friends, knowing that you are safe and that no lower energies can get near you! No energy vampires can get to you!

Advanced and primitive civilisations

We here on planet earth think we are very advanced, with all our modern technology.

But what if I told you that we are actually very primitive? What if I told you that there are civilisations millions of light years ahead of us? What if I told you they see us in the same light as we see the ants and the tiniest creatures on our planet? What if I told you that instead of advancing we are actually going backwards?

Let's first consider the meaning of *advanced* civilisations and *primitive* civilisations.

Is an advanced civilisation simply a civilisation that has lots of modern, advanced technology? We have advanced technology! Does that mean we are an advanced civilisation?

Alternatively, is a primitive civilisation one that has no advanced technology? But with no technology, surely that must mean closeness to Nature and a greater awareness of all living things? Is a civilisation such as this, primitive? Or could it actually be an advanced civilisation?

If so, then are we here on planet earth advanced or primitive?

Advanced civilisations are those civilisations who share

everything. No one goes without. Everyone's needs are met. Are we an advanced civilisation?

Advanced civilisations are those civilisations where the rule is not the survival of the fittest. Everyone is respected and valued. Are we an advanced civilisation?

Advanced civilisations are those civilisations where all forms of life are respected. Killing is not looked upon as a sport. All life is protected. Are we an advanced civilisation?

Advanced civilisations are those civilisations where everyone knows that there is ample for everyone. There is no desire to hoard or take more than you need, because you know there is always plenty. Are we an advanced civilisation?

Advanced civilisations are those civilisations who understand that everything in the entire cosmos is connected. There is no such thing as separateness. What affects one affects all. If I hurt or offend someone, then I am doing that to myself. So therefore I am very careful about how I treat other people. Are we an advanced civilisation?

Advanced civilisations are those civilisations where there is complete respect for Mother Earth and gratitude for what the universe freely provides. There is no need to compete to get what we want. We just need to let everything come to us in Divine timing. Are we an advanced civilisation?

Advanced civilisations are those civilisations who have very advanced and sophisticated technology which is used for the betterment of all. We have nuclear power. That's very advanced. What do we use our nuclear power for? To help everyone? For the betterment of all? Are we an advanced civilisation?

So, how did we score?

Or did we even score at all?

Do you still think we are an advanced civilisation?

Let's now look at those higher energy level civilisations that you read about earlier.

Those life forms on other planets and in other civilisations do not do war, violence, crime, hatred, anger or any of the negative activities we seem to spend our time here on planet earth doing.

Those life forms on other planets and in other civilisations do not live separate from each other or from God. They all know their true nature is Divine essence. They all know they are all One in God Energy. Therefore there is utmost respect for everyone and for all forms of life.

Those life forms on other planets and in other civilisations do not compete with each other to gain power or possessions. They all know there is ample for all.

Those life forms on other planets and in other civilisations do not lie or deceive or manipulate each other to achieve their own ends. And why not? Because they are so highly Spiritually evolved that they do not communicate with words, but with mind telepathy. Their thoughts are their words! That means no one can deceive or lie as everyone is a mind reader.

Those life forms on other planets and in other civilisations have technology far more advanced than we could ever imagine. That's because their minds and souls are so highly advanced, and because they are so connected to their Source, their Source of Divine Energy. And because of that, their highly advanced technology serves them.

With us here on planet earth, however, it is the other way around! We are slaves to our technology! Yes, we have all the gadgets, all the equipment, all the machinery, all the modern devices, most of which are meant to make life easier for us. But look what has happened! All those gadgets have got to be paid for! So most of us spend all the hours we can, working in order to pay for them! We don't have time to stop and admire the sunrise ar sunset any more. We don't have time to admire and enjoy the beauty of Nature. We don't have time to just sit at peace with ourselves in the quiet and calm, replenishing and nourishing our soul. We don't have time to give attention to those who need help, either here or in other parts of the world. We don't have time for our friends, just hanging out with them doing absolutely nothing.

Walk down any street in any town and what do you see? Most people are on their mobile phones! Completely unaware of their surroundings! So much so that they keep bumping into each other! It's like an assault course trying to work your way down a main street!

Even the joggers and walkers! They have their headphones plugged in, totally disconnected from all the beauty in Nature around them! People in a restaurant! At least one at every table is on the phone! So much for conversation! They may as well have stayed at home! Even there, the television and computers have taken over our lives!

But! Worst of all! We have given our power away! We have given our power away because it suits us to do so! It suits us to let other people work things out for us and tell us what to do. We are too busy rushing everywhere trying to catch up with our tails that we have allowed other people to dictate to us, people who want to control and manipulate us for their own ends.

We live our lives in a frenzy! *Do, do do! Go, go, go! Have, have, have! Get, get, get!*

Life is not meant to be a frenzy! We are meant to be happy and at peace with ourselves! Just like as on those other vibrations where all the life forms know only love!

So you see, we are very primitive indeed, compared to all these other civilisations who are so far advanced from us that we cannot imagine what life must be like for them.

All these advanced civilisations exist on a much higher vibration or dimension than we do here on planet earth. In fact, we here on planet earth are the infants in the whole story of creation. We have a long way to go!

And the main difference between us and the highly advanced civilisations is, of course, that we have developed our technology and our material possessions at the expense of our Spiritual development. We have sacrificed the Spiritual in favour of the physical! We have lost sight of the beauty of Nature; we have lost sight of our Divine Essence; we have lost sight of the fact that we are all connected, we are all One.

And look where this neglect of our Spiritual development alongside our technological development has got us! A divided, decimated, fractured world! There must be something wrong with the way we are doing things! There must be something seriously wrong when there are numerous other far more advanced civilisations than us, civilisations with far more advanced technology than we can ever imagine, civilisations who live in peace and harmony, in total Oneness, total unconditional love, while we kill and torture each other, destroying not only ourselves, but our planet as well!

What is wrong with us? How can we continue to miss what is so obvious? How can we fail to see that when we break our connection with our Divine natural essence, we destroy ourselves and our world? How can we continue to fail to acknowledge that our soul development must parallel our technological and physical development? The two must go together! A civilisation cannot advance if there is no corresponding Spiritual development!

That's why advanced civilisations are just that! Advanced civilisations! Simply because, with them, the two go together!

They are Spiritually advanced as well as every other way advanced. That's why they live in peace and harmony with themselves and with the entire cosmos!

How much longer before we primitive people here get the message?

And yes! We are being watched! Not in an unfriendly or threatening way! Remember, we here on planet earth are the only ones who do war, violence, anger, manipulation and greed! We have a monopoly on all of that! Charming!

We are being watched out of curiosity and in absolute amazement and even disbelief.

How can those people on planet earth treat each other the way they do? What is all this war and killing all about? Do they not understand we are all One? How can they destroy their beautiful planet? How can they take more than they need and leave many without? Do they not understand there is more than sufficient for all? How can they lie and deceive so much? Do they not understand that there can only be truth? Why do they hate so much? Do they not understand the meaning of love? What is going on there? Just look at them all! What has gone wrong with them? They have all this technology, but they are using it to kill each other! They need help!

And we are also being watched with not just a little apprehension! We are being watched by civilisations that are so far advanced than us in technology that they could wipe us out completely! But we are the only ones who do wiping out! Remember? Wiping out is not the way of advanced civilisations! Right?

What are they going to do next? What new bomb are they going to explode? Do they not realise that we are all connected? Do they not understand that whatever they do on planet earth affects us all in the entire cosmos? Are they going to destroy the entire cosmos? They are all so sad! Perhaps we should help them? Should we make contact with them? What if they try to kill us? We do not kill, so what will we do? We cannot allow them to destroy everything in the entire cosmos! What can we do?

So, do you still think we are an advanced civilisation?

Really?

CHAPTER 13

Angels and Archangels

Angels have been known to us for centuries, and have featured in all religious traditions. Like us, angels too are evolving, and their upward development depends on how well they do their job with us. They are beings of pure light, and are with us now at this time in greater numbers than ever before, to help in this massive shift in the earth consciousness and the Spiritual evolution of all humanity.

You read about how 2012 was so important in shifting all the energies in the entire cosmos, and how earth's vibration itself was raised as a result of the re-aligning of the planets. You have learned too that as a result of earth raising its energy vibration, new higher vibrations are now able to reach earth. So it is that angels are now flocking to all corners of the earth. They surround us with loving acceptance and non-judgement, seeing us all as the bright shining light, the spark of Divine Essence that each of us truly is.

Everything is now changing, and the universe is re-arranging itself to adapt to that change. When we connect with the angels, we expand and grow in our own Spiritual development, and we become closer to the realisation that we are wonderful beings, spreading love and light around our beloved planet earth.

Angels are very high, Spiritual beings, operating on a much faster, higher, energy vibration than humans, and, unlike humans, they have never incarnated on this earth. They are mostly androgynous, which means they are neither specifically masculine nor feminine, as their masculine and feminine aspects are in perfect balance, though they can, of course, take on the appearance of either. They are God's messengers, an extension of the Divine, here to serve humanity and to guide us and protect us on our Spiritual path. They always radiate love, peace and compassion. Because their vibration is so pure and high, they are invisible to most of us, except for those of us whose vibration is high enough to enable us to see them. Otherwise, we can experience them through a feeling, a sensing, a knowing that they are all around us, a soft, glowing, loving, peaceful feeling that cocoons us.

A white feather is a very strong Spiritual sign, the calling card of an angel. Many people find these small, soft, white feathers in the most unusual places. When you find a small, white fluffy feather, know that an angel is with you, and acknowledge that angelic presence, there to comfort you and let you know that everything is fine, you are not alone.

You just have to think of angels in your mind, and they are

there immediately. What they cannot do, however, is intervene in your life without you asking them. You have to invite them in, we all have free will, and the angels cannot and will not impose themselves on us without our prior asking. Also they will not interfere with us learning the lessons we have come here to learn. They are here to help us fulfil our life's mission, and our Higher Self's purpose. They will not stop us being irresponsible, they will not make our decisions for us, and they will not take away an illness if it is a part of our life's plan. They will comfort and guide us, they will watch over and protect us, but they will not lead our lives for us. They will remind us of the task we have taken on, as they know all about our life plan that we ourselves created. They can ease our stress and make our path less difficult, if we listen to them.

In order to tune into our angels, we need to raise our energy vibration. We raise our energy vibration by not holding on to feelings of hatred, anger or fear, and by replacing them with the higher vibration feelings of kindness, compassion, caring, forgiveness and gratitude. This opens us up to be more receptive to our angels' messages. Our diet also is important, replacing lower density foods such as meat and sugar with less dense substances such as fruit, vegetables, seeds and nuts. Many animals die in trauma, and so, if we eat that meat, then we are absorbing that trauma. If we stop eating meat, stop smoking, stop drinking alcohol and stop taking any kind of drugs, then we are fine tuning our bodies, making it much easier for the angels to connect with us.

GUARDIAN ANGELS

We each have a Guardian Angel who is with us throughout all of our lifetimes, joining us in the womb or at the moment of birth, and accompanying us through each of our incarnations. As we cross back to Heaven again at the end of each lifetime, it is our Guardian Angel who guides us back safely into the Light. Our Guardian Angel knows absolutely everything about us, our needs, our moods, our thoughts, our strengths and weaknesses, and, of course, all our previous incarnations. Our Guardian Angel is always with us, waiting to do our bidding, but only if it is for our highest good.

What a beautiful, magnificent being your Guardian Angel is! And you have this beautiful, magnificent being all to yourself! Your Guardian Angel is here for you! Nobody else! Just you!

Your Guardian Angel sees you as the beautiful Spiritual light you really are, perfect in every way. Your Guardian Angel is your best, most constant and loyal friend. Your Guardian Angel does not judge, criticise or chastise you, ever. Your Guardian Angel is constantly supporting you, never giving up on you, never deserting you, no matter what you do.

What a wonderful, beautiful, amazing gift each one of us has in our own Guardian Angel!

ARCHANGELS

Of all the many different hierarchies of angels, it is the Archangels we know most about. This is because the Archangels work closely with our earth energy vibration.

Perhaps you have also heard of Seraphim, Cherubim or Dominions? These are higher ranking angels, and they work with those other civilisations you have read about who exist on a much higher energy vibration than we here on planet earth.

Now let's meet the Archangels!

Firstly, **Archangel Michael**. You have already learned about Archangel Michael when you were learning how to protect yourself. Call on Archangel Michael for strength and protection, as he is the Archangel of protection. Archangel Michael's colour is blue, and his blue cloak will always protect you and keep you safe.

Secondly, **Archangel Raphael.** Call on Archangel Raphael for healing for yourself or others, as he is the Archangel of healing. Archangel Raphael's colour is a beautiful emerald green, the colour of healing.

Thirdly, **Archangel Gabriel.** You probably recognise Archangel Gabriel as the angel who told Mary that she was to be the mother of Jesus. Archangel Gabriel's colour is white, and you can call on him to help you communicate better with others, or to help you to receive the messages from your angels.

Fourthly, **Archangel Uriel.** Call on Archangel Uriel for peace and tranquillity in your life, and ask him to help you to send out the right energy to attract to you what you need. Archangel Uriel's colour is a beautiful gold and purple.

Fifthly, **Archangel Anael.** Archangel Anael will help you to love yourself more, and will also help you with all kinds of relationships.

Next, **Archangel Jophiel.** Call on Archangel Jophiel for more Spiritual knowledge and wisdom. Archangel Jophiel's colour is yellow.

Archangel Chamuel is the Archangel of the heart. So of course, Archangel Chamuel's colour must be pink! Ask Archangel Chamuel to help you see everyone with unconditional love, and to fill you with unconditional love for yourself and all humanity.

Archangel Zadkiel removes all negative energy with his Violet Flame. Violet is the strongest healing colour and changes all negative energy into more positive energy. Ask Archangel Zadkiel to remove all negative energy from your aura. Yoo know what negative energy in your aura leads to! And you definitely don't want that! So ask Archangel Zadkiel to clear it all away.

Archangel Raziel will give you a greater understanding of the Spiritual laws of the universe. These are the rules of the game of life! You will learn more about these laws in chapter 17 and how important they are in the game of life. Archangel Raziel will help you to live by these laws, so your life will run very smoothly and calmly.

Archangel Metatron is the archangel who holds all the geometric and mathematical equations and designs of the entire cosmos all together. Ask Archangel Metatron to increase your light energy and to cleanse and re-energise all your chakras. Archangel Metatron will also help you to understand more clearly about all the higher dimensions and vibrations.

Finally, **Archangel Sandalphon** will strengthen your connection to Mother Earth. Ask Archangel Sandalphon to help you connect with the little elemental spirits and energies in Nature.

These are the best known of all the numerous archangels. So now that you have met them, you can call on them at any time. They are always on duty, 24 / 7!

With all of these mighty beings of light, you are never, ever alone!

Got that?

You are never, ever alone!

CHAPTER 14

Spirit Guides

As well as having a Guardian Angel to watch over you and protect you, you also have some Spirit Guides.

So who are your Spirit Guides? And what is the difference between your Spirit Guides and your Guardian Angel?

Firstly, unlike your Guardian Angel, who has never incarnated in this world, Spirit Guides have reincarnated time and time again. They have now gained enough brownie points to be able to remain on the vibration of Heaven and act as helpers for us here on this earth vibration.

Secondly, unlike your Guardian Angel, who remains with you throughout all your life-times, your Spirit Guides change over time, depending on the lessons you are trying to learn, or according to your needs at any given time.

Perhaps you have acted as a mentor in school for another student? That means you were helping them, looking after them and being there for them, guiding them along a certain path.

Well, that is what your Spirit Guides do for you. They are your Spiritual mentors who have already learned the earthly lessons you are still trying to learn.

Your Spirit Guides never judge you or criticise you. They are with you to comfort you and support you on your chosen path through this life-time. Your Spirit Guides are always arranging various synchronicities to make sure you are always in the right place at the right time. They encourage you to see yourself as the co-creator of your own life, and to take responsibility for your own actions.

Remember you learned about how you return to Heaven after each life-time? How you decide if you want to return to earth and then start to work on the plan for your next life?

Well, if you have collected enough brownie points, then you might well decide to stay in the higher vibration of Heaven and help others still here on earth. That means that you would then be a Spirit Guide to someone else, helping them along their path from your vantage point in the higher vibration of Heaven.

Listening to your Spirit Guides is a very wise thing to do, simply because they are there to help you through your life's plan. If you work alongside them your life will run so much more smoothly and peacefully.

When you sit quietly and connect with your inner self in meditation, that is when your Spirit Guides can get through to you. Go with your intuition and thank them for their constant help. You are never alone!

CHAPTER 15

The Elemental Kingdoms

It's all about energy again and how different energies vibrate at different frequencies.

You know now there is an intelligence, an awareness, in every living thing. That is God intelligence, God energy. You know too that we are all part of an overall, great collective intelligence that seeks to express itself in many realities and in many forms.

Every flower, every tree, every rock, every blade of grass, every plant, every stone, every river, every ocean, every bird and insect are all an expression of the God energy, just like you. And as you know, they are all various expressions of God, in order for God to experience all life.

Nature is throbbing with life, both in what we can see with our eyes, and with life on higher energy vibrations, where we cannot see just quite so easily.

This life all around us in Nature, on the higher vibrational levels, which we cannot see with our limited human vision, is what we call the '*Elemental Kingdoms.*'

It is here that the fairies, elves, pixies, gnomes, sprites and other beings exist who are all involved in helping Nature to grow.

Yes! They all do exist!

It is here too in these higher vibrational energy frequencies, in the subtle worlds that you now know make up our connected vast universes and cosmos, that unicorns and dragons also exist.

Yes, unicorns and dragons do exist!

Your great grandparents and those before them knew all about the fairy creatures who inhabit our landscape. Earlier generations long ago were very much in touch with the intelligence in every living thing, and that did not just mean the *tooth fairy!*

So why are we not still in touch with these fairy, mystical, other world energies today, energies that are still around us just as they were for earlier generations? Life forms that still cry out to us for recognition! Life forms that have so many lessons to teach us! Life forms that can help us earn so many brownie points!

You know the answer to that!

You know that we have lost contact with all this wealth of magical, wonderful, colourful, creative, pulsating, dancing, singing forms of energy because we are no longer tuned into their frequencies. We are no longer able to make contact with them because our energy vibration is too heavy, too slow, too dense! They cannot get through the thick veil that we have built around ourselves with our noisy life styles, our always having to *do, do, do; go, go, go; get, get, get.* We are no longer able to '*just be'*. We are contaminated and absorbed by all the modern, advanced technology now available to us. But, as you learned in a previous chapter, modern, advanced technology does NOT create an advanced society! As you learned in a previous chapter, you need soul development as well; you need growing Spiritual awareness; you need increasing Spiritual consciousness as well as just new machines and modern technology.

And you know what has happened to us! We have developed all this technology without a corresponding growth in our Spiritual Awareness, without an expanding awareness of our connection to Divine Source. So we have ended up using all this wonderful technology to kill each other instead of using it for the betterment of everyone. How sad is that? What have we done? We definitely need help!

And there is an unlimited supply of help and healing offered to us from the Elemental Kingdoms!

From your science classes, you probably know about the four elements that make up all of life. These four elements are water, earth, fire and air. And again, it's all energy! Each of these four elements has elementals and fairies looking after it, all working to a highly structured plan, caring for it and making sure it can do its job.

The water spirits, who work and heal using the power of water, are called *undines, sprites* and *sylphs.* When you stand quietly and watch a gushing stream flowing past, and if you listen very carefully, you just might be able to hear the laughter and squeals of sheer delight of the water sprites as they tumble down over the stones, racing each other in the flow of the water. You might even see little sparkling lights flashing past you. That is just the little water sprites, undines and sylphs having fun!

The earth and air elementals look like *Tinkerbell,* with transparent wings and energy shapes which look like bodies and which change colour depending on what they are doing and where they are.

The fairies who work with fire energy are called *Salamanders,* very powerful and very magical! Watch a young child stare into a fire or a candle flame. Remember what you read about young children and babies who have just recently arrived from Heaven and how their energy is still high and pure, as they are still in touch with all things magical? Well, they are watching the salamanders dancing in the flames of the fire. Maybe you too can see different coloured lights flashing and moving about in the flame? That's the salamanders having fun, dancing and swirling in all their colours.

And, of course, all these forms of life have an aura of their own. That universal energy that vibrates in all of us and shows in our aura also vibrates in all of Nature and in every other form of life.

The human eye can be trained to see this energy surrounding each living thing. Using your peripheral vision, look just beyond the edge of a tree or plant or the top of a mountain. Soften your gaze, and you will see a grey coloured mist, a haze surrounding the life form. That is the aura of that particular life form. With practice, you will begin to see it more easily.

Perhaps you already can see auras around people or flowers? That means your energy is vibrating at a high enough frequency for them to make themselves visible to you! Lucky, lucky you!

They are on a higher vibrational frequency than us, so it is always their decision, not ours, as to when they allow us to see them. When you are ready, it will happen!

Your garden is a truly magical place! Each plant and tree, each flower and blade of grass has its own spirit looking after it. To connect with the spirit of a tree, give it a personality. That means try and imagine what that tree would be like if it was a person. Every tree and flower has its own unique personality, and in connecting with that personality, you are actually connecting with the spirit of the tree, with the elementals that look after and care for it, that help it to grow by pouring their essence into it.

So that explains why all trees and plants are different and why all the flowers have different colours.

What makes each one different is the spirit looking after it, pouring its own energy, its own essence, into it, giving it strength and nourishment and helping it to grow to fruition. That beautiful colourful flower is the essence, the expression of the energy of the elemental looking after it. God co-creating with the elementals! God energy expressing itself through the elementals and into the flowers. Creation of life-forms! Never-ending! God continuously creating! God doing what God does! Creating and experiencing that creation! Remember you learned all this earlier in this book? See how everything fits into the great universal energy that we call God?

So go on, hug that tree! And then the next one, and the next! Feel the energy passing from the tree to you! That's the energy of the elemental, the fairy, looking after that tree!

You are connecting with the magical kingdom of the elementals! The fairies are working through the central stem of the plants, the trunks of the trees, pouring in their own beautiful essence, giving each tree, each flower, a bit of their own personality, a bit of their own character, a bit of their own consciousness.

Yes, there is a loving, Divine plan at work constantly, holding all forms of life together in the most exquisite, the most elaborate design! What a plan! What a tapestry! What a design!

The greatest show on earth! That's Nature and the elementals who work with Nature!

CHAPTER 16

Famous Nature Poets

Nature is constantly calling out to us, constantly trying to catch our attention, constantly just looking for acknowledgement.

Do you ever stop and admire the flowers? The first snow-drops that tell us spring is on its way? That field full of daffodils or tulips that display so much beauty? That little primrose growing on the bank by the road-side? The tiny buds on the trees showing the growth of new life? The rainbow after the rain?

Do you ever stop and listen to the bird-song? Their chirping and tweeting as they gossip amongst themselves? The gushing of the river tumbling down over the stones? The waves lapping onto the shore? The wind sighing through the trees? The rumbling of the thunder?

Do you ever listen to the rain? Do you ever just sit and listen to the whole orchestra of the combined raindrops, each creating a different sound, a different note, as they land melodiously on each leaf, each blade of grass, each tree, each roof-top, each puddle?

Do you ever notice the aroma of all the different plants, shrubs and flowers? The intoxicating fresh smell after a shower of rain? The smell of the potatoes just dug out of the earth? The sweet scent of a field of freshly cut corn or freshly cut grass?

Do you ever walk in your bare feet on the grass and feel its softness? Do you ever let sand pour through your fingers? Do you ever feel the velvety softness of a leaf or a petal? The solidness of the trunk of a tree?

Do you ever watch the sun as it sets in a spectacular display of colour each evening? Do you ever watch as it creeps over the horizon each morning? Do you ever watch the moon and imagine what it is like up there? The stars as they twinkle in the night sky?

Are you aware of the cycle of Nature in the changing seasons, with all their colour and splendour? The new life in the buds in spring? The fullness of the trees and all the colours of the flowers in summer? And of course, the grand display of colour in autumn, as Nature bows out in a magnificent grand finale, before taking her long winter rest, to return again the following spring, refreshed and renewed?

The colourful display of the autumn leaves! The kaleidoscope of swirling, dancing, pulsating colours and energy in the dark ruby reds, bright crimsons, sparkling greens and jades, deep scarlets, copper golds and speckled yellows! A truly magical show of splendour and magnificence!

The purity and magic of Nature's winter coat of white, draped over her shoulders! The shimmering, sparkling, glittering landscape of the fairy land created by the frost and ice!

Down through the centuries, poets and writers have all written about Nature and the lessons Nature is constantly teaching us.

Having now read this book, you have learned so much about your own nature, the nature of God and all the other dimensions and energy vibrations surrounding us in the entire cosmos. You know a lot more too about the Elemental Kingdoms and Nature. And you know that there is an intelligence in all living things.

The great poets and writers all down through history knew all about this Great Intelligence in all living things, and were very much in touch with it.

So now, let's take a closer look at some of these most famous Nature poets, and see if you now understand the meaning of their words.

First, let us consider the words of the famous poet John Donne, who lived in the late sixteenth and early seventeenth centuries.

John Donne wrote: "*No man is an island, entire of itself*".

Can you figure out what this means? Remember what you learned about us all being one and all being connected? And about us all needing each other and how, if we hurt someone, then we are really hurting ourselves?

Well that is exactly what this poet is saying! And you can now see how it is true!

John Donne also wrote about how death does not actually exist: "*Death be not proud, though some have called thee / Mighty and dreadfull, for thou art not soe / For those whom thou thinkest thou dost overthrow/ Die not, poore death, nor yet canst thou kill me / Why swell'st thou then?*"

You have probably noticed that some of these words are spelt differently from the way we spell them today. The language, too, is not just the same as ours. That's because John Donne lived a very long time ago, over five hundred years ago, in fact! People then used different words from us so that's why you might find John Donne's language strange. But you understand what he means!

You have learned about energy and how we are all energy, constantly changing form. You have also learned that when we finish our life here, we do not cease to exist, we just change energy form. In this famous poem, Donne is speaking to death and telling death it has no need to be proud because it does not actually exist. In fact, it is death itself which in the end will die! *"Death, thou shalt die!"* So now you can understand what Donne is saying here!

Consider too, these words of Donne: *"I am a little world / Made cunningly of elements."*

Donne was very aware of all the subtle worlds in our connected cosmos! Just as you too, are now aware of all the different energies, energy vibrations and different dimensions that go to make up the entire cosmos.

See how you can now easily understand a lot about John

Donne's poetry!

Now let us look at another very famous poet, William Wordsworth, who lived from 1771 until 1850. Wordsworth lived at a time when the Industrial Revolution was changing the way in which people lived their lives. The Industrial Revolution was the bringing in of new machines to do the work man had previously done by hand. New factories were built, and they brought a lot of smog and pollution with all the smoke belching out of their chimneys. Wordsworth lived in a very beautiful area of England called the Lake District, where he was surrounded by all the beauty of Nature. He was one of the first of the Romantic poets. These are poets who loved Nature and lived very close to Nature. In fact, Wordsworth called Nature his "*Nurse*" and his *"Mother".*

Wordsworth's most famous poem is his '*Ode on Intimations of Immortality'.* An ode is an address to someone or something expressing how you feel. So Wordsworth is dealing with *immortality* here, and the fact that we never die, our soul is immortal.

Can you see what Wordsworth is saying here?

First, he explains how, "*Not in entire nakedness / But trailing clouds of glory do we come / From God who is our home."*

Then he explains how our birth *"is but a sleep and a forgetting",* and how our soul, *"that rises with us, our life's star, hath had elsewhere its setting / And cometh from afar".*

At our birth, a veil of forgetfulness is pulled down over our eyes, because if we were allowed to remember that "*celestial light",* that "*imperial palace whence we came",* the whole plan for our life here on earth would fall through, there would be no point whatsoever in us coming here. Wordsworth says how *"Heaven lies about us in our infancy"*. Remember reading about how young children and babies have just come from Heaven and are still in touch with their friends there? Well that is exactly what Wordsworth is saying here! We know our existence has changed, though, from what it was like in Heaven, and as we grow older, we forget more of that previous existence as we settle into our life here on earth once more: *"Turn whereso'er I may / By night or day / The things which I have seen I now can see no more."*

However, even as we grow older, we are still aware of who we really are and of our Divine essence. We are very much aware of the Universal Consciousness of God, that Universal Energy, *"A presence that is not to be put by / A motion and a spirit that impels / All living things, all objects of all thought / And rolls through all things."*

Exactly what you have learned in this book! How the God Energy is in absolutely everything!

Wordsworth wrote another very famous poem called *'The World is too much with us'*.

Can you tell what this means?

Can you tell what he means when he says: *"We lay waste our powers / Little we see in Nature that is ours; / We have given our hearts away, a sordid boon!"*

This is what you read earlier about how we have become slaves to modern technology, and how we are looking in the wrong places for happiness. Here we are with all this modern technology, but we have lost touch with Nature! We have made a very bad deal for ourselves!

Wordsworth understood perfectly how all life forms in Nature are constantly in contact with each other: *"Ye blessed creatures, I have heard / The calls ye to each other make!"*

So you see how Wordsworth's poetry all fits in with what you have learned in this book!

Now let's look at another famous poet, Gerard Manley Hopkins, born in 1844. The title of one of Hopkins' famous poems, *'God's Grandeur'* explains itself. He puts it very simply: "*The world is charged with the grandeur of God!*"

Well, having read all about the nature of God and what God does, you can see very easily what Hopkins means by this! How the God Energy is in everything! How God creates everything!

Hopkins also wrote: "*Look at the stars! Look, look up at the skies! / O look at all the fire folk sitting in the air! / The elves' eyes!*"

This is a clear and direct reference by Hopkins to the magic in the Elemental Kingdoms that he could see all around him in Nature. Just what you read about in this book!

Hopkins also saw how "*Nature is never spent*".

This is easy to understand! Nature keeps renewing itself all the time, and there is an unending supply providing enough for everyone.

Hopkins appealed for us to have more respect for Nature in

his poem '*Binsey Poplars*'. Do you know what an '*analogy*' is? Perhaps you have learned about this in your study of literature? An analogy is like a metaphor, where you use comparison to get across your message. Hopkins uses an analogy to get across his message about how we damage the environment. He compares damaging any part of Nature or the environment to damaging your eye. Your eyeball is a very sensitive part of you, and if you damage your eyeball in even the slightest way, then you will damage your whole eye, and therefore also your sight: "*A prick will make no eye at all.*"

In other words, Hopkins is telling us that if we damage any part of Nature, we affect all of Nature. Again, something you have learned in this book! What affects one aspect of Nature, affects all aspects! And why? Because we are all connected! We are all One! That's why!

Hopkins appeals to us to stop destroying Nature by cutting down all the trees and green areas. In his famous poem '*The Windhover*' ('*To Christ our Lord*'), he challenges us: "*What would the world be, once bereft / Of wet and wilderness? Let them be left / Wilderness and Wet / Long live the weeds and the wilderness yet!*"

You have just read about all the little elementals in Nature busily working away to help all the flowers and trees to grow by pouring their spirit, their essence, into them. So when you cut down trees or destroy the green areas, you are destroying the little elementals who exist there!

Have you ever noticed how lifeless your garden or the countryside seems in winter? Have you ever wondered why this is?

This is simply because all those little energies, in the form of fairies, elves and pixies have gone back into Mother Earth for the winter. In other words, they have withdrawn their energy from the garden. That's why it seems so lifeless. Then, when spring returns, their energy returns too, and the whole place comes alive with life again!

Next time you cut your grass, try this experiment and see what happens! Before you cut, ask the *little folk* to withdraw their energy for a while to allow you to cut the grass. Show them respect by telling them you know you are on their territory and you do not want to hurt them while you are cutting the grass. Notice how a stillness, a sort of eerie feeling hangs over everything! That's because they have left! Then, when you have finished, ask them to come back again. You will sense the life returning to your garden! That's because they are bringing their energies back!

Show respect to them, too, by not using pesticides and chemicals in your garden! That really hurts them!

All Nature asks for from us is respect and acknowledgement. Not much to ask for really, when we consider all the joy Nature gives us!

Perhaps you have read the novel '*The Colour Purple*' by Alice Walker? Perhaps you have actually studied it for your exam?

If so, then you will remember how the character Shug says: *"Everything want to be loved. We sing and dance, make faces and give flower bouquets, trying to be loved. You never notice that trees do everything to git attention we do, except walk?"*

Again, the same character says: *"I think it pisses God off if you walk by the colour purple in a field somewhere and don't notice it."*

Another character, Celie, admits: *"I never truly notice nothing God make. Not a blade of grass (how it do that?) not the colour purple (where it come from?) not the little wild flowers. Nothing. Now that my eyes opening I feels like a fool."*

You now understand what all this is about!

The trees, the plants, the flowers and everything around us in Nature have their own support mechanisms, they are all self-sustaining. All they want from us is just to be acknowledged, to be shown respect, to be loved. The sad thing is that many of us do not even notice Nature, nor do we acknowledge all that planet earth does for us.

It is Celie too, who tells us*: "We go to church to share God, not to find God."*

You know what this means! That God is everywhere and in all things! And you know what Celie says is true! You don't have to go to church to find God. God is in every form of life all around you. All you have to do is look! And, of course, God is in you!

Celie asks the question *"What God look like?"*

Even before you now read Shug's answer to Celie's question, you know what the answer is going to be! But you didn't know the answer before you read this book! See how much you have learned? See how much wiser you are? See how much more aware you now are of all things Spiritual?

You understand Shug's explanation: "*Don't look like nothing. It ain't a picture show. It ain't something you can look at apart from everything else, including yourself. I believe God is in everything. Everything that is, or ever was, or ever will be. And when you feel that, and be happy to feel that, you've found it..........But one day, when I was sitting quiet and feeling like a motherless child, which I was, it came to me: that feeling of being part of everything, not being separate at all. I knew that if I cut a tree, my arm would bleed. And I laughed and I cried and I run all around the house. I knew just what it was. In fact, when it happens, you can't miss it.*"

Is this all not exactly what you have learned in this book?

William Blake, another famous poet, saw natural beauty and God in everything*:* "*To see a World in a Grain of Sand / And a Heaven in a Wild Flower / Hold Infinity in the palm of your hand / And eternity in an hour.*"

Now let me remind you of something else you have learned! Remember reading about how our modern technology has taken over our lives? How all this wonderful technology is not really so wonderful after all? How it has cut us off from Nature?

Let's consider the poem, '*Cynddylan on a Tractor*'*,* written by R.S.Thomas, born in 1913. Thomas is showing how a mechanical machine is disturbing the peace and quiet of the rural areas and how man is no longer connecting with the soil, as the machine is now doing that for him. Cynddylan is a *"new man now"*, the gears of the tractor *"obeying his least bidding"*, as he rides out of the farm-yard *"scattering chickens"* and *"emptying the wood / Of foxes and squirrels and bright jays"*. He is so caught up in his new tractor that he no longer notices how *"the sun comes over the tall trees"*, or how *"all the birds are singing, bills open in vain"*.

You can very easily see how this all fits in with what you have learned earlier. We allow ourselves to get carried away with all the new technology, not realising that we are disconnecting further and further from Nature and all that really matters.

In another of his poems, '*Farm Child*', Thomas describes a young boy who lives on a farm and whose world revolves around Nature. His head *"is stuffed with all the nests he knows"*, his pockets are full of *"flowers, / Snail-shells and bits of glass, the fruit of hours / Spent in the fields by thorn and thistle tuft."* His treasures! The final line *"Earth breeds and beckons"*, sums up Thomas' message that we can never be comfortable with material possessions, to which so many of us are falsely attracted.

So, what conclusion have you reached?

Have you decided that man is taking note of Nature and learning the lessons Nature is trying to teach us?

Or have you come to the conclusion that man is not in tune with Nature at all?

This poem, '*Wagtail And Baby*', by Thomas Hardy, another poet who lived in the late 19th century, and was very aware of Nature, might help you decide.

"A baby watched a ford, whereto / A wagtail came for drinking; /A blaring bull went wading through, / The wagtail showed no shrinking. / A stallion splashed his way across, / The birdie nearly sinking; /He gave his plumes a twitch and toss, / And held his own unblinking. / Next saw the baby round the spot / A mongrel slowly slinking; /The wagtail gazed, but faltered not / In dip and sip and prinking. /A perfect gentleman then neared; / The wagtail, in a winking, / With terror rose and disappeared; / The baby fell a-thinking."

Have you got the message the poet is trying to get across to you?

A "*blaring bull*" and a "*stallion*" are certainly not animals you would want to meet face to face. They are ferocious! Yet, neither of these, nor indeed, the *"mongrel"* disturbed the bird in any way. However, when the "*perfect gentleman",* the very best of men appeared, what did the bird do? It rose in "*terror and disappeared"!*

So, as you can see, we humans are not exactly looked upon with trust by the other forms of life with whom we share this planet earth! We are feared! And all because of our actions!

Just like Celie in 'The Colour Purple', whose eyes were opened, your eyes too have been opened in so many ways! You cannot go back to being as you were before you read all this! And that is a good thing! Think of what all those people who do not know what you now know, are missing!

Finally, let us consider another very famous poet, Robert Browning, who lived from 1812 until 1889, and is considered one of the greatest poets of the Victorian period of history.

You may have heard of him before as the writer of '*The Pied Piper of Hamelin*'. In his famous poem, *'Paracelsus'*, Browning sums up for us a lot of his own Spirituality and his own beliefs. Can you now identify with what Browning is saying? Do you now understand what he means?

"Truth is within ourselves; it takes no rise / From outward things, whate'er you may believe, / There is an inmost centre in us all, / Where truth abides in fulness; and around / Wall upon wall, the gross flesh hems it in, / This perfect, clear perception- which is truth."

In the same poem, Browning also writes:

"What God is, what we are / What life is--- how God tastes an infinite joy / In infinite ways........ God joys therein!..........God tastes a pleasure".

Remember what you learned about what God does? How and why God creates? Is Browning not saying the same thing here?

So you see, many poets right down through history have been telling us all along about God, about life and about why we are here. They were all very strongly connected to their Spiritual body, their soul, and so they had a very deep understanding of all things Spiritual.

And now, you too have a greater understanding of what these great poets and writers have been expressing in their works! You now understand the messages they are trying to get across to us! And you have learned all this from just reading this book!

PART FIVE

PLAYING THE GAME!

CHAPTER 17

The Game of Life

Now you know all about who you really are, where you have come from and why you are here. You also know about the nature of God, all about energy, reincarnation and what happens when you pass back again to Heaven after each lifetime here on planet earth.

You can now see the vastness of all of creation and how we are all One in that vast creation and all connected, both spatially and lineally. *Spatially connected* means we are connected to every other living thing around us and *lineally connected* means we are connected to all the people who have lived before us, all our ancestors and forefathers, and to all who will come after us. And why? Because we are all made from the same God energy!

And now you also know how absolutely everything in the entire cosmos, all the planets, all the stars, all the other eleven universes besides our universe, are all connected. You are aware too, that what happens here on planet earth affects every other part of the cosmos.

You also know about the '*vibrational corridor*', the '*cosmic elevator*' the '*vibrational highway*', and how there are countless other civilizations in existence in other vibrations, many of them millions of light years ahead of us.

So, let's consider all of this!

Let's put your life here on planet earth into perspective!

That examination you did last week, or last month, or last year! It just did not go very well for you. In fact none of your exams have gone very well for you! You expected to do better. Perhaps you have even failed the whole lot!

So what? So what does it matter in the overall scheme of things? What does it matter in the whole vastness of creation? What difference is you failing your exam going to make in all of that?

None! Absolutely none! Absolutely no difference whatsoever! It does not even appear on the radar screen!

And here you are getting yourself all worked up and upset about an exam! Getting yourself upset and worked up over something that has absolutely nothing whatsoever got to do with the reason why you are here on planet earth! If you did not pass that exam, then you were not meant to pass it! It was not for you! It is not part of your life-plan that you yourself created for yourself! Get over it! Get over yourself! Move on!

What about that detention you got last week? Is that going to shake the foundations of all Creation? I hardly think so! Not even a bleep on the screen!

What about that driving test you have just failed? Is that going to bring everything in creation crashing down on top of us? I don't even need to answer that!

Maybe you are in trouble because your bedroom is an utter mess! Again! Maybe your bedroom is always in a mess?

So what? You are the one sleeping in there! It's your mess! That's normal teenage stuff! And again, your bedroom mess is not going to register as a huge event of great importance in the whole vastness of creation, is it? All the other civilisations in the entire cosmos are hardly going to investigate your messy bedroom! It's just you being you, and just you being you is what you came here to planet earth to be!

All you can do is try your best. All you can ever do is try your best. In fact, as you now know, by trying to push yourself towards a certain outcome, a certain result, you are most probably interfering with the universal flow of energy! Remember what this is? The universal flow of energy is the flow of energy that brings to you everything you need.

In actual fact, all you ever need to do is be happy! How difficult can that be? Just do whatever it is you really love doing, and love the things that you do! That's it in a nutshell! That's the whole big secret of life! Being true to yourself! Living your life as just you and nobody else!

If you do not want to go on to further education, if you want to spend your life working at a particular trade which does not require a university degree, then why would you push yourself to extremes to get into university? You will not be happy doing something you do not enjoy! Happiness only comes from doing what you enjoy doing! Happiness does not come from a highly paid job, no matter how many degrees you had to obtain in order to get that job! Happiness can only come from you being at peace with yourself, doing what makes you happy, and not taking on a particular career just to make someone else happy or just because it is expected of you!

The universe knows exactly what you need, and is doing everything to get that to you, at the right time. By you trying to achieve a certain outcome, an outcome that might very well not be the outcome for your highest good, then what are you actually doing? You do not know what is for your highest good. What you desire for yourself is not the same thing as what is for your highest good. But the universe knows what is for your highest good! The universe knows exactly what you need! And the universe is always sending that to you at the right time. So when you try to produce the outcome you desire, you are actually interfering, you are actually blocking the universal energy from delivering the right thing to you!

So chill out! Relax! Take it easy! Life is not meant to be struggle and hardship! Life is meant to be a game of fun! A fun game of learning! Finding the clues, joining up the dots, fitting the pieces of the puzzle together!

Just go with the flow!

Remember, everything, absolutely everything and everybody in your life you yourself have chosen, to help you to learn the lessons that you yourself chose to learn.

If you are living in a family where there is violence or cruelty or neglect of any sort, then remember, you have got to look for the lesson behind all of this! You yourself have chosen to be in this situation so that your soul can evolve through experiencing all of this. This is all for your own good, for your own soul development!

Perhaps there is illness in your family? Perhaps your mum or dad has already passed back to Heaven again?

Remember, they have their life-plan too! If they have passed back to Heaven, then that means they have already fulfilled the function they agreed to play in your life. Your paths will cross again, your lives will be connected again! Your lives are always connected! Of that you can be absolutely certain! They have not gone anywhere. They have not left you. They are simply on a higher vibration than you are right now. But when the time is right, when the right time comes, you too will be on that vibration and they will be waiting for you! You will all be together again on a higher energy vibration. And remember too, they are still aware of what you are doing here on this earthly vibration! They are still helping and guiding you from their vantage point in that higher vibration, where they can now see everything, unlike you here on earth where you have only very limited vision. They can see the whole picture, while you can only see a very small part of the picture.

So, you can see that there is a reason for absolutely everything! There is no such thing as a chance or a coincidence! There is only '*synchronicity*'.

Synchronicity means the coming together, in perfect timing, of all the elements necessary to produce a perfect outcome for your highest good. The universe has been at work! The Universe is always at work! Working to get the best outcome to you! The universe is not going to send you anything harmful. You do not need to get involved! Just let it all happen! Just go with the flow! The flow of universal energy! Just accept and watch as everything unfolds around you in perfect timing! Perfectly timed delivery from the great universal energy!

Playing by the rules

So, life is a game!

Like all games, it's not the winning that is important, it's the taking part.

But like all games, though, there are rules to be observed, and all players need to know these rules, otherwise the game would be an absolute shambles, an absolute free for all!

So let's take a closer look at these rules. Let's take a closer look at the rules for the game of life that will help you to play this game and succeed.

Remember, though, there is no competition here! You are not competing with anyone else. There are no losers in the game of life! You are here to play out the scenario you yourself planned for yourself in your life's blue print. And if you do not get it completed this time around, you will have many more chances to do so!

Think of it like a great big maze! Think of the fun you have trying to find your way through it! And it is never about who gets out first! It's just about getting there! It's about all the fun along the way!

So, what are these rules? The laws for the game of life are called the '*Spiritual Laws of the Universe*'.

In your physical life, there are laws you must abide by, and if you break those laws, you could end up in prison or given a hefty fine.

But you know that God does not judge and God does not punish. There is no court of law for you to face if you break any of the Spiritual laws. All it means is that you are hampering your own development, you are making it harder for yourself to earn brownie points. If you observe these Spiritual laws, it means life will flow easily and more plentifully for you! You will have an abundance of everything! And if everything is coming to you easily and in abundance, then why would you ever think of not living by these laws?

So, let's start!

Let's find out what these laws are!

Let's look at these laws which, if we adhere to them, promise us an easy and abundant life.

Let's see how we can go with the flow!

The Law of Giving and Receiving

As you give, so you shall receive. What you give out, you will get back in a greater amount. As you sow, so shall you reap. Treat others as you would have them treat you.

You have heard all this somewhere before!

It's not exactly rocket science! It's simply the universal law of giving and receiving. What goes around, comes around.

The entire universe functions and operates through *giving* and *receiving*. Everything must be kept flowing in continuous movement. This is an abundant universe, but all must be kept flowing and circulating. Whatever we stop flowing or circulating, then we stop its circulation or flow back to us. If we hoard money, for example, then we are stopping the flow of money back to us. Money, like everything else, must be kept in circulation. The more you keep the flow of anything going, the more of that will come back to you.

When you pay your bills, do not do so begrudgingly, as that causes a blockage in the flow of positive energy. Bless your bills as you pay them, giving thanks for the service you have enjoyed, and thanking the universe for providing you with the money to pay. Now you increase the flow of positive energy. And you know where it is headed! Happy days!

When you give from your heart, with unconditional love, not asking or expecting anything in return, then you immediately set in motion an unstoppable flow of energy that must, by Divine Law, bring a return to you, multiplied many times. How good is that?

Every time you go to visit someone, bring a gift, no matter how small. When you feel someone is having a bad day, give them a gift. It does not always have to be something material. How about a hug? A smile? A compliment? Good wishes? A pleasant greeting? Then just watch as a miracle unfolds before your very eyes! Just watch as a great ripple starts to unfurl and spread from you to them and out beyond them to everyone else they meet! What you have just done here is, you have raised their vibration, by making them happy, and they are raising the vibration of others.

See the power you have?

Never ever underestimate the power of the ripples you create! The ripples you create by just a smile, a caring word, a helping hand! As Mother Teresa said: *"I alone can't change the world, but I can cast a stone across the waters to create many ripples".*

And don't forget! You '*give*' in your thoughts as well! You have seen how every thought, every word, is a form of energy, and once a thought or word goes out from you, it sets in motion an irretrievable effect, making it materialise in the exact form you '*gave*' out.

So send out happy thoughts, good intentions, kind words, and you will increase the flow of positive energy in the universe! Send out thoughts of anger, envy, greed, hatred, revenge, and you will only increase the toxic, poisonous energy already out there! And you know what will happen! It will all come back to you multiplied!

" *Oh Horror! Horror! Horror!"* Remember Macbeth's words?

Whatever you *give* out, in either physical or mental form, you will get back.

And you need to be willing to *receive* as well! Remember, energy circulates! It does not just keep on flowing in the one direction! So if you keep *giving* and not *receiving*, then you are blocking the flow. You must be willing to *receive* as well.

You must be willing to *receive* all the abundant gifts the universe is constantly sending you!

Remember what I told you about going to school with a sulky, cross face? That sulky, cross face means you are not willing to accept or *receive* any of the gifts the universe is sending to you today! You are really losing out! Big time!

I'm sure you know people who *take* everything and *give* nothing or very little back. These *takers* are not living in the higher vibration energy of love, where one knows that this is an abundant universe, with ample for all. These *takers* are blocking the flow of natural abundance to everyone.

You do not need me to tell you how the world is divided into those who have very little and those who have so much they don't know what to do with it all. This is because the *taking* and the *giving* in the world is not balanced. The *takers* are blocking the flow of everything good to everyone else. It all needs to be balanced. There is sufficient for everyone, but the *takers* keep blocking the flow by *taking* more than they need, hoarding what they have *taken* and not *giving* back.

You remember how the energy you *give* out attracts like energy back to you? Well, don't forget that if you *give* out negative energy in the form of fear of being burgled, or being sick, for example, then you are actually attracting the burglar, you are actually attracting the sickness to you! It's the law of giving and receiving! There are no exceptions!

If you give out thoughts of having no money, then you will block money coming to you. If you give out thoughts of having money, then you will attract money to you! If you give out thoughts of ill health, then you will attract ill health to you. Everything, absolutely everything you give out by thought, word or action, will attract the same back to you, multiplied.

As I said, there are no exceptions!

As you *give,* so you shall *receive.* What goes around comes around. Treat others as you would have then treat you. As you sow, so shall you reap.

That's the rule of *giving and receiving!*

That's the game of life!

The Law of Gratitude

We are all part of a great big Spiritual jig-saw!

Every person you meet, everything that happens to you has been planned or orchestrated for a reason. And that reason? To help you learn the lessons you yourself have chosen to learn.

So you must show gratitude for absolutely everyone and everything that comes your way! And this includes the negative! Especially the negative!

Do not hold grudges against that person who has caused you hurt or pain! Instead, thank them for the part they have played in your life and for the lesson you have learned from them.

And now move on!

Remember, you are here to learn, and when someone or

something is no longer serving your life's purpose, it exits from your life, leaving way for something greater and better to emerge.

Give thanks for absolutely everything in your life! And when you give out thoughts and words of gratitude from your heart, then you know what happens! The universe returns your gratitude with more of the same!

It's just like when you give someone a gift. If they express sincere gratitude, then how does that make you feel? It makes you feel you want to give them more! Alternatively, when they show no appreciation for your gift, then how does that make you feel? It certainly does not encourage you to give them anything, ever again!

So it is with the universe. If you express gratitude to the universe for all the wonderful gifts constantly flowing into your life, then the universe will continue to flood your life with all good things. The universe will increase the flow of energy back to you.

That's the law of gratitude!

That's the game of life!

The Law of Forgiveness

It can often be very difficult to forgive those who insult us or who are unkind to us, or who hurt us in any way.

But that is exactly what we must do! We must forgive!

Of course, we have free will, so we always have a choice. We can choose not to forgive.

But let's consider what happens when we choose not to forgive; when we choose to go on holding a grudge against someone; when we choose to continue to feel bitter and resentful towards someone; when we continue to hold feelings of anger and thoughts of revenge.

Well, first of all, you know that all these feelings and thoughts go out from you in the form of energy. And you know what energy going out from you does!

The energy you send out attracts more of the same energy back to you! And what good is that going to do you? Will all this horrible energy coming back to you make you feel better? I don't think so!

Secondly, is there not already too much negative and toxic energy out there without you adding to it? I think you know the answer to that one!

So, if you choose not to forgive, is that really a good idea? When you think of how you are not exactly helping the situation, only making it worse, then it cannot really be a good idea!

So the other choice you can make is to *forgive*.

Now let's see what happens when we choose to *forgive*.

When we choose to *forgive*, we are playing a very clever game!

When we choose to forgive, we are actually helping

ourselves! We are releasing ourselves from the burden of carrying that hatred and bitterness around with us. It is like taking an enormous weight off your shoulders! And that is exactly what forgiveness does! When you forgive someone, you are relieving yourself from all that weight you have been carrying around with you, all that burden which has been like a chain around your neck! All that hurting that has been like a great dark cloud hanging over you. You are freeing yourself from that hurt and from the past.

So, instead of sending out more toxic fumes and energy, we can send out compassion and love in the form of forgiveness. And that is what will disarm those who have offended us! If they find we are not reacting to them, then they cannot continue to fight with us! An eye for an eye and a tooth for a tooth will only result in the whole world being blind and toothless! Brilliant! Just brilliant! That's all we need!

These people need our love and affection, not our anger! They must be hurting in some way to do what they are doing! So they need love and compassion, not more of the same!

Now, remember what you learned about us all being One? How I am you and you are me?

Well just think about that now!

Why would you want to hit back at yourself? Why would you want to get revenge on yourself? Surely you can see, that just does not make any sense!

And there is another great reason for why you should not hold grudges against anyone, another reason why you should forgive.

What are those thoughts sending out? Where will those thoughts go? What will those thoughts turn into?

Yes! Exactly! Those thoughts of revenge, anger and bitterness that you are sending out will all come back to you in the form of negative energy! Negative energy multiplied!

It's a heavy, dangerous, sharp boomerang this time!

OUCH! THAT REALLY HURT!

And yet another reason why you should forgive is because, as you have already learned, you do not know anyone else's life plan or the role they are here to play. We can never judge, as you now know, because everyone in our life is helping us to learn a lesson. Those people who perpetrate evil and horrible sufferings on others are giving us the opportunity to learn the lessons of forgiveness and compassion. And if we react by giving out more of the same? Well, it's good bye to those precious brownie points again!

So you can see how the pieces of the jig-saw all fit in together!

You can see how the dots all join up!

You can see that life is a game!

And you can see how to play it!

The Law of Karma

The Law of Karma affects each and every one of us, with absolutely no exceptions.

Karma is NOT a punishment or a judgement.

Karma is simply a balancing. A balancing of all our actions.

There are two types of actions: good actions and bad actions. There are two types of karma: good karma and bad karma. Good actions create good karma; bad actions create bad karma. Good actions and good karma contribute to future happiness; bad actions and bad karma contribute to future unhappiness and suffering.

You read in the last section why you must forgive and not hold grudges against anyone.

Well, another reason why you should not hold grudges or try to get revenge on anyone is simply because you don't need to!

And why not?

You do not need to try to get revenge on anyone because karma takes care of all that for you!

Let me remind you here of two very important lessons you have already learned. First, you have learned that *we are all One.* Secondly, you have learned about *reincarnation.*

Because we are all one, we have a big responsibility to make sure that our actions do not hurt or offend any other person or any other form of life. If we do hurt anyone, then that bad action has got to be balanced out by some good action on our part. We must make up for our bad actions in some way.

Remember too, what you learned about *reincarnation?* How we keep coming to this earth plane to learn the lessons we want to learn? And how, if we don't learn them in this life-time, we will try again in another life-time?

Well, karma has also got to do a lot with reincarnation and why we keep coming back time and time again.

We keep reincarnating in order to make up for some of our bad actions, in order to balance out our karma.

Say, for example, in our last life-time here we were very cruel to animals or we exploited children. Then we have got to make up for that. So in this life-time we might be here to work on behalf of animal or children's rights. Or we might have shown no sympathy or understanding to our alcoholic father or mother in a previous life-time. So now, in this life time, we are that alcoholic person ourselves, here to make up for our previous lack of understanding and lack of compassion.

Get the picture?

Karma is, as you can now see, another reason why we do not need to try and get revenge on anyone for hurting us.

The law of karma is another piece of the jig-saw just slotting into place. Another piece of the jig-saw of life!

Another part of the game of life!

EPILOGUE
LIFE IS BUT A GAME!
GO WITH THE FLOW!

Now that you have read this book, you cannot go back to who or where you were before.

And why not?

Because you now know too much! That's why!

Because you have now changed your beliefs about who you really are, your beliefs about God and your beliefs about life! That's why!

Because you now know that you and God are One. You now know that you are One with everything and everyone else in the entire cosmos! You now know that there is no such thing as separateness or no such thing as individual pursuits for individual glory. You now know that we are all intrinsically connected both spatially and lineally, with all forms of life. What affects one, affects all. You now know that you are here to increase your own Spiritual awareness and the Spiritual awareness of all mankind. That's why!

Because you now know that life is eternal, with no beginning and no end! You now know that we are all part of the Great Universal Energy, the great Divine Intelligence that continually seeks to experience itself through continuous creation. That's why!

You now know, too, that God is not going to change anything except *through you*. You now know that *you are a co-creator with God* in the continuing evolution of life. You are an integral part, a vital part, a key player, in the creative process of Nature and evolution.

You know too, that this is a very messed up world and you know why it is so messed up. You know this world is so messed up because we keep trying to fix it by changing the conditions. Because we keep thinking the solutions lie in economics or in politics.

We have now come to the end of a long cosmic cycle, and we stand on the brink of a new age for mankind.

As always, we have a choice. We can choose to develop or to destroy, to progress or to regress.

Our problems are neither political nor economic. Our problems are Spiritual problems. So therefore, the solution must have something to do with our Spirituality and how we see ourselves in the overall plan for humanity.

As long as we continue to try and change the world through just trying to change the conditions in the world, we are never going to get anywhere. As long as we continue to try and make these conditions just disappear, we are never going to get anywhere. As long as we continue to think that all our present conditions can be sorted out by money or war, we are never going to get anywhere.

We have been doing all this down through history! And the result? This fragmented, fractured, divided world in which we now find ourselves! Not much for all those thousands of years of work! Huh?

If our track record is anything to go by, then we cannot even be trusted to change a light bulb, never mind to change the world!

We must be doing something wrong! There must be something we are missing out on! Something we are failing to see!

You now know what we need to do! What *you* need to do!

You now know that we need to *change the beliefs that have created* these present conditions in the world. You know that the present intolerable conditions are the *result, the reflection, of our beliefs.* Our greatly mistaken beliefs! We first of all need to *change people's beliefs* and then *their behaviour will change.* It's not rocket science! It's just common sense! But the problem is, common sense is in very short supply in our world right now!

We have got to change our beliefs! That's the key to finding the solutions! That's the secret!

And as we change our beliefs, then political systems, educational systems, monetary systems, religious institutions and all other systems must inevitably change.

And you have started this process!

You have changed your beliefs about who you really are, your beliefs about the nature of God and where God is in our world, and your beliefs about the nature of life.

And because you have changed your beliefs, you will now

change your behaviour!

You now believe that this is an abundant world, with plenty for everyone. You now believe that we are all One and we all need each other; there is no separateness or division. Our current issues of world hunger, world poverty, war, greed, violence and injustice all stem from our mistaken belief in separation from one another, separation from Nature and separation from our Divine source.

You now believe that we are Spiritual beings, a spark of Divine Essence, having a physical experience in a physical body for this life time. You now believe that we are here to learn certain lessons in order to advance our soul, and we will come back time and time again until we learn those lessons.

You now believe that you have great power. You have great power because you are of Divine Essence, because you are of God. You have power too through knowledge. Knowledge is power. And the fact that you have now got this knowledge at an early stage in your life is what is bringing hope to the world.

You have been awakened to the truth at an early age for a reason. You must now awaken others. You must awaken others to the truth about their beliefs.

You are starting on a new path in your life. This is the path of truth, hope and love.

You are starting to live your life in truth, hope and love. Armed now with all this knowledge, you have all this power to change our world.

You are the future generation, the future rulers of the world. You have the power to change the world!

You have the power to change our world into a world where all people are free to be and to do their best, where all people can fulfil their own inherent inner calling, bringing forth each person's individual genius, each person's individual creativity, each person's individual talents, each person's Spirituality, co-creating for the betterment of all, and unrestricted by the dictates of societal or institutional beliefs and teachings. You are born creative, endowed with free will and creative talents, and you have an inalienable right to express your creativity, but also an inalienable responsibility to express your creativity for the betterment of all.

You are going to have fun. You are going to have fun because you know that in having fun, you are spreading laughter and happiness. You are creating powerful ripples that will reach out further and beyond where you can ever imagine.

So cast your pebbles! A smile, a friendly word, a kind helping hand, that's all it takes to start a tsunami of change.

You are going to change beliefs. You are going to show others that this life is a fun game, and when you know the rules and play by them, then you create a wonderful, rewarding life for all of us.

You are going to show others that life need not be full of sorrow and suffering. You are going to show others that we live in a loving universe that knows exactly what we need and is delivering. You are going to show others that life is not meant to be a struggle. Life is meant to be easy, and it is easy, if we just go with the flow!

When we go with the flow we are accepting that there is a deeper plan, a greater power beyond us, that has everything in control. This does not mean we sit back and do nothing! Rather, this means that we continue to do our best, in the full knowledge that we are supported and helped, and knowing that we do not have to struggle to make things happen according to our desired outcome. We sense we are being guided and co-ordinated by the *Whole,* of which we are an integrated part.

You are going to change all the suffering and tears of sorrow into tears of joy. You are going to change attitudes. You are going to change the media from a disaster-obsessed media into a good-news media. If people around the world see the good that is going on in our world, then they will naturally want to be a part of it.

You are going to change scientific discoveries into advances for bettering our world instead of destroying it. You are going to develop educational systems that build and manage the world's most valuable asset, the world's young people. You are going to develop educational systems that nourish and foster our connectedness with every form of life in the entire cosmos.

You are going to play a vital part in this great planetary awakening that is affecting all mankind. You are going to co-create with Divine Intelligence and with Nature to restore harmony and balance to our unbalanced world.

So do you now see why you freely chose to re-incarnate at this particular time?

You have chosen to be here now in order to play a vital part in this great awakening that is taking place and gathering momentum right across planet earth. This great awakening process that is unstoppable, unalterable, indefatigable.

The world needs you!

You are going to be busy!

So start now! Let your new beliefs spread outwards from you to others. Let your beautiful soul light shine out to others. Let your unconditional love for everyone show them that they can live a life of peace, harmony and abundance.

Go now, and use your power wisely, for the betterment of everyone!

Enjoy your next great adventure!

You have the power!

You *are* the power!

Play the game of life! Go with the flow!

NAMASTE!

Eileen McCourt

Made in the USA
Charleston, SC
16 March 2016